TYING
AND FISHING
THE TERRESTRIALS

Also by Loring D. Wilson:

The Handy Sportsman
The Edge of the River

TYING AND FISHING THE TERRESTRIALS

Loring D. Wilson

SOUTH BRUNSWICK AND NEW YORK: A. S. BARNES AND COMPANY

LONDON: THOMAS YOSELOFF LTD

© 1978 by A. S. Barnes and Co., Inc.

A. S. Barnes and Co., Inc.
Cranbury, New Jersey 08512

Thomas Yoseloff Ltd
Magdalen House
136–148 Tooley Street
London SE1 2TT, England

Library of Congress Cataloging in Publication Data
Wilson, Loring D
    Tying and fishing the terrestrials.

    Bibliography: p.
    Includes index.
    1. Fly tying. 2. Fly fishing. I. Title.
SH451.W56   688.7′9   77-74113
ISBN 0-498-02069-X

PRINTED IN THE UNITED STATES OF AMERICA

To
Carl Bracken and Gary Toulouse,
whose observations on fly-fishing for bass and panfish
have filled in a few important gaps
in the study of the terrestrials

CONTENTS

TYING
AND FISHING
THE TERRESTRIALS

1
THE TERRESTRIALS

In the history of fly-fishing and fly-tying literature, the great bulk of research and information has been given over to the order Ephemeroptera, most commonly known as mayflies, and constituting those aquatic insects which provide the flytier and fisherman with the dramatic hatches that have been the subject of several notable books. The purpose of this book is not to denigrate the value of the mayfly hatches or the authors who have so admirably commemorated them, but rather to examine a field that has hitherto been unjustly neglected by most of the fishing authors—the terrestrials.

Terrestrials are those insects which are common to the land, and which do not undergo their metamorphoses beneath the surface of the trout waters. It is primarily because of this fact that they have been overlooked, although most fishermen realize their value, as witness the number of general fly-tying books that mention them briefly in passing. The disadvantage to those books is that they present at the most eight to ten patterns, and expect the flytier (especially the novice) to add these patterns to his boxes of mayfly imitations, simply in order to be a well-rounded angler and prepared for the "possibility" of using them, "when the mayflies aren't rising." But few tiers use these patterns to advantage, for the simple reason that they have been constantly inundated with the belief that the *best* imitator patterns are those which are adapted to the hatches of ephemera.

Nothing could be farther from the truth. The fact is that, while the ephemera hatches are certainly dramatic, and cause the trout to go on massive feeding sprees when they are present, the classic *Iron fraudator* is lucky to get a rise when the real insects aren't on the water en masse, because they seldom if ever hatch one at a time, and

11

trout, being selective creatures with a modicum of intelligence, are not used to seeing a single fly of that variety on the water. The only way in which the fly can possibly be effective, except in the middle of a hatch, is to create an "artificial hatch" by making many floats over the fish, and attempting to dupe him into believing that there is a natural hatch going on. Unfortunately, this seldom works, and even when it does, it takes up so much of the fly-fisherman's time in concentrating on the single fish that it can hardly be said to be worthwhile. In a like situation, with no insects on the water, a good ant imitation would probably bring a rise on the third drift.

For the past two years, I have experimented extensively with the terrestrial patterns, to the complete exclusion of all mayfly patterns from my boxes. In that time I fished the same rivers, streams, lakes, and ponds that I had frequented in years before, and fished no more frequently than I had in previous years. According to my stream diary, my success averaged slightly better for the two-year period than when fishing with the mayflies, and on some days in late summer the difference was astounding—for example, on August 13, 1969, fishing with a variety of mayfly patterns, I caught and released three trout of seven inches to nine inches in length on Laurel Run in Southwestern Pennsylvania; on August 15, 1974, on the same stream, but fishing ants, crickets, and a green deer-hair worm, I caught and released fourteen trout of seven inches to eleven inches, and took two additional one-footers home for dinner. The time on the stream was from two P.M. until dusk on both days.

This certainly is not to say that the mayfly patterns are without value. They have caught fish consistently since Theodore Gordon's time, and will continue to do so until the last trout has been choked to death by the chemical effluvia of our civilization. But matching the hatch is a pain in the rod butt. And for the fisherman who just wants to go out and capture a few trout, matching the hatch can be a time-consuming and frustrating experience that detracts from rather than adds to the enjoyment of his craft. On the other hand, when fishing the terrestrials, the angler can readily determine, if there are in fact insects floating in the surface tension, whether they are red ants, black ants, sowbugs, or grasshoppers, and he doesn't need the home-grown degree in entomology that so many of the angling writers seem to have acquired. However, for the flytier anxious to improve his craft, the terrestrials are still available for collection and study, and are much easier to capture and examine than the various forms of minutiae that the ephemera men rely upon.

Over the past two years I have discovered four dozen patterns that have proved consistently effective in taking trout, panfish, bass, and even some brackish-water marsh-dwelling species of fish not commonly sought after by the brotherhood of the junglecock, but which provide some excellent sport, especially in the dog days of summer. Those patterns will be covered in the following chapters, but, if you feel like going on, don't stop with these. Capture a few insects of your own and work out some patterns. The forty-eight terrestrials described here will teach you the proper techniques for imitating these important trout foods, and will prove effective in ninety-eight percent of fly-fishing situations for those fish which eat them; I leave it up to you to provide the other two percent success.

Since the terrestrials are fished in a slightly different manner than are the ephemera, a section of the book will be devoted to the art of using these creations, for trout, bass, panfish, and brackish-water fishes. As with the chapter on tying tools and materials, the fishing section will deal with the proper tackle and accoutrements for use in fishing the terrestrials, and the remainder of that section will concentrate on special methods for the different fishes, and for the different types of water in which they are found.

Terrestrials, while not the most dramatic of the trout foods, are certainly one of the most important, and the consistent use of terrestrials will revolutionize your angling success. The difference in food value and attractiveness between an *Iron fraudator* and an *Amblytropidia occidentalis* grasshopper is approximately that between a slice of processed American cheese and a two-inch steak, and the choice is obvious.

The entomological information on the various insects is provided, both in a general chapter on identifying insect characteristics and, for the individual insects themselves that are covered herein, immediately preceding the tying instructions for the patterns. In addition, I have provided a separate chapter on the collection and preservation of terrestrials, so that the fisherman with a desire to learn more about these important creatures can undertake a study of them, and further his knowledge while furthering his enjoyment. On the other hand, for the angler who simply wants to catch some fish without a great amount of study and work, these patterns will more than suffice in themselves. After all, the most important thing in any type of fishing is to enjoy what you are doing, no matter how simple or complicated you make it.

2
TOOLS AND MATERIALS

There is no getting around it; the tools and materials for fly tying in general are specific, and one cannot "make do" with poor quality or improper action in either category. While the tools utilized in tying flies in general are the same as those used for terrestrials, it is perhaps wise to go over them for the fisherman who desires to begin tying flies with this book. In the realm of materials, there are far fewer materials needed in the tying of a complete complement of terrestrial patterns than in tying the mayflies or the other traditional patterns, and rather than attempting to give a complete range of the materials used by the tyers who deal with all sorts of patterns, the material section of this chapter will deal only with the various furs, feathers, and miscellany necessary for the tying of the patterns in this book.

TOOLS

VISE: The most important tool in fly tying of any sort is the vise; there is simply no way that you can get by without a good one. The little stamped metal vises that come with fly-tying kits aren't worth the time it takes to take them out of the box and throw them away. Even if you begin with a less expensive vise, you will end up getting rid of it as you get into more sophisticated tying in favor of a better one, so the four- to five-dollar vises available from Herter's and a few other companies are still a waste of money.

The major characteristics of a good vise are jaws that can hold a fairly wide range of hook sizes, ease of adjustment of the jaws, the ability to adjust the vise for height, and speed of operation. The last can be sacrificed for the beginner, but again, as you progress you will

14

want the greater speed, and this is found only in cam-actuated vises.

There are a few really good vises on the market that have all of these characteristics, and notable among them is the Thompson Model A vise. Currently, the list price of this vise is approximately $16.00, but most of the fly-tying materials companies discount this cost somewhat, so that the vise will actually cost you between $12.00 and $14.00 depending upon the individual catalog. I have used a Model A vise exclusively for the past sixteen years, and a few drops of oil on the moving parts twice a year have kept it in perfect shape. The jaws handle hooks from size 26 to 1/0 without trouble, and that is quite a range.

Thompson also has what they term the Ultra vise, listing at around $21.00, the only difference between it and the Model A being the fact that the Ultra is adjustable for collet angle. I personally don't consider this feature as being worth the extra money. The standard angle of fly-tying vises has sufficed for so many years that I strongly doubt it could be improved upon. Then there is the Model B vise, having the same sized jaws as the above, but with the collet closed by means of a wheel at the tail of the vise. In addition, it is not adjustable for height, and although it costs a few dollars less than the Model A, the lack of the cam and the height adjustment eliminate any value in the savings. Thompson also makes a few other styles of vises, but they are not designed for the person who really wants to tie up all of his own flies—they are beginners' vises, less expensive, and without the features that make a vise really effective.

There are also a few vises available in this country from Veniard of England. Like much of the English fly-fishing and fly-tying gear, these tools are excellently crafted and well worth the money, although they do tend to cost more in general than the Thompson vises. The three most notable are the Salmo vise, excellent for larger flies, the Coulsdon midge vise, and the Croydon hand vise. These, at least, are the most commonly available in this country. There are several other models available from Veniard's directly, of which the Cranbrook most closely approximates the Thompson Model A, and retailing for approximately the same price. However, one must calculate the cost of shipping into the total cost of the vise, and because of the greater shipping costs from overseas, until the Cranbrook is offered by some of the companies in the United States, it will cost more than the Thompson. Both the Coulsdon and the Croydon are currently available from Fly Fisherman's Bookcase and Tackle Service, and the Croydon is available from Dan Groff's Rod and Reel; the cost of the Coulsdon is about ten dollars, and the Croydon is priced at less than five dollars from either company. While these are excellent vises for tying the minutiae, such as the #20 ants and the #24 thrips offered in this book, they have the disadvantage of having the jaws closed by a collet on the jaws themselves, much like a pin vise, and therefore

15

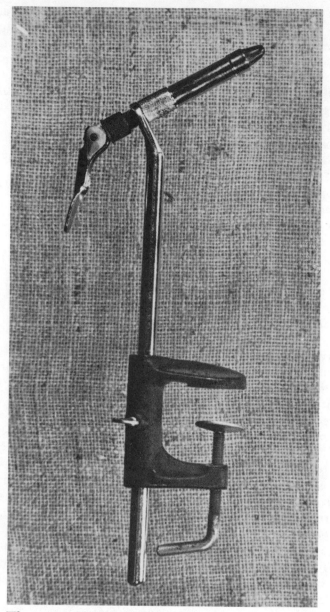

Thompson Model A Vise

are dreadfully slow—in short, they are a specialized tool for a specialized aspect of fly tying.

SCISSORS: Next in importance in the flytier's collection of tools are scissors, and once again these are specialized tools for the purpose. They must be sharp as a razor and finely adjusted for clipping something as wispy as a single hackle fiber; they must taper to a very fine point, and, most important, they must cut all the way to the point; and they must have relatively large finger holes so that they will be comfortable in use. Good quality embroidery scissors fulfill all requirements with the exception of the large finger holes, and they will do in a pinch; however, all of the fly-tying materials houses offer excellent scissors for between two and four dollars, and since you will be paying that for good quality embroidery scissors, you may as well get the ones designed for fly tying.

Most tiers have two pair of scissors (at least), a very fine, delicate pair for trimming hackle, thread, and the like, and a heavier pair for cutting bucktail and tinsel, two jobs (among others) that will throw a delicate pair of scissors out of alignment almost as fast as a hammer will. I purchased two pair of fly-tying scissors from Herter's approximately six years ago, and they are still working as perfectly as they did the day I received them. Herter's is currently undergoing some price fluctuations, but at this time the scissors are selling for about $2.40 for the delicate scissors and $2.60 for the heavy-duty scissors, and those prices, for the quality, would be hard to beat anywhere else.

If you decide to use embroidery scissors, purchase those made by Wiss or another reputable manufacturer—not the little Italian scissors in the polyethylene packages on a rack in the supermarket. Those packaged scissors, unaffectionately termed "El Cheapos" by flytiers, will go out of alignment after a dozen flies, and since in most cases they are riveted together rather than screwed together, they can't be readjusted. Purchase decent quality to begin with—in a craft such as fly tying it pays off in the long run.

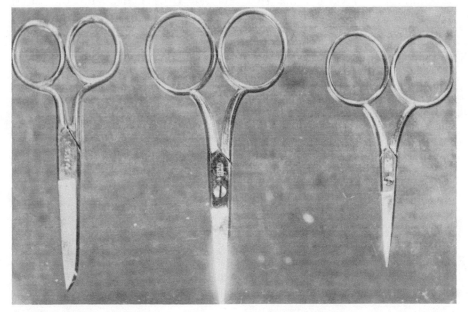

Fly-Tying Scissors

HACKLE PLIERS: The final, absolutely required commercial tool, hackle pliers are essential for the proper construction of a hackled fly. They come in several styles, and it will be best to look at a few of them.

First and foremost, there is the traditional English-style hackle plier, consisting of forged wire on the shape of a spring, the jaws being flattened so that they overlap and containing striations or scoring to give a good grip on the hackle. All fly-tying companies offer some variety of the English style, the prices ranging from a dollar to about $2.50. They come in two different sizes, the so-called standard, and the "trout size" or midget variety. Both have their advantages, although I have found that for tying the terrestrials the trout size is all that is required. If you are going to be tying some other, larger flies as well, get both sizes. The one problem with the English-style pliers is that if the serrated jaws are too sharp they have a tendency to cut the hackle, since the spring tension is quite strong. If you have trouble, fold a piece of fine emerycloth in half, grip it with the pliers, and pull it back and forth between the jaws, just enough to take the edges off the serrations, but not enough to remove them completely.

Herb Howard hackle pliers, offered by some companies, are a variation on the English style, with slightly less tension and longer, finer jaws. They are excellent for hackling smaller flies, and I have never had any problem with their cutting the hackles, probably due to the fact that there *is* less tension on the jaws.

Then there are the pliers that, generically, I call the stamped pliers. These are formed from a strip of spring steel, and the jaws are made of various materials affixed to the metal strip. Generally, the most common of this variety has two serrated rubber pads for the jaws. These pliers are very inexpensive and, amazingly enough, excellent in quality. Just about every company offers either the Thompson variety or a duplication of their own. Thompson also offers Duplex pliers, in which one of the jaws is rubber and the other is serrated metal. These give the cushioned effect of the all rubber-jawed pliers, but the extra grip of the metal-jawed English style. In addition, Herter's offers pliers with a rubber jaw and a brass jaw consisting of circular grooves rather than transverse serrations. None of these pliers will take a great deal of pulling, but the Herter's pliers, at least in my experience, seem to slip off the hackle more easily than do the twin rubber jaws or the Thompson Duplex pliers. Since this variety is so inexpensive, you can easily order a pair of each and try them out yourself. If you only want two pairs of pliers, I strongly recommend one pair of the double rubber-jawed variety, and a second pair of either the Herb Howard or the trout-sized English pliers.

BOBBIN: The bobbin is simply a thread holder that contains a spool of prewaxed thread and pays it out as needed. It also serves to keep

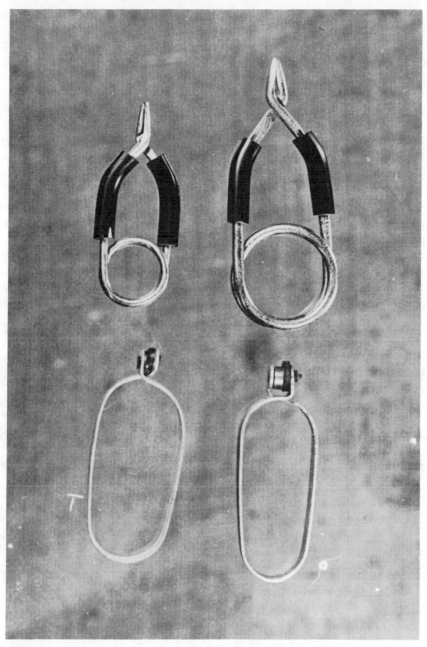

Hackle Pliers

Small English   Large English
Nonskid   Duplex

the thread under tension while tying, and, if your hands happen to be rough or calloused, it prevents the callouses from fraying the thread. Bobbins come in a wide variety of shapes and styles, not to mention cost, ranging from $1.25 to about $4.00, and in a wide variety of complications. If you want a bobbin, get a simple one, one that will take standard spools of thread (some have their own spools that have to be prewound—a definite pain in the neck) and that is quite simple to take apart for changing thread color. If your hands aren't too rough, simply cut a length of thread and tie it with your fingers, using a wooden, spring-type clothespin to hold the thread under tension while performing other operations.

RAZOR BLADE/SCALPEL: A single-edged razor blade or a doctor's scalpel is a handy, if unnecessary tool, for the flytier. It is used to cut off thread when finishing up the fly head, among other operations—the thread is held under tension and the razor blade brushed lightly against it. It will cut the thread off closer to the head than will scissors, and offers the added advantage over scissors of not cutting the hackle, which will simply bend away from the blade.

Doctor's scalpels are somewhat easier to use, and can be purchased

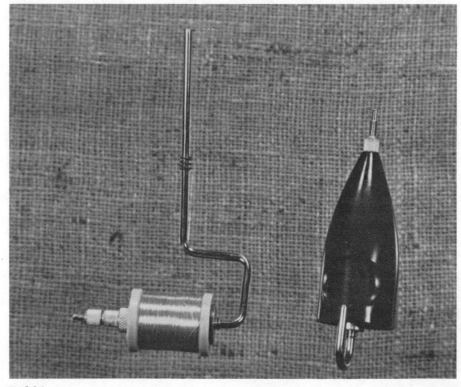

Bobbins

for a dollar or so at biological supply houses, and through some of the fly tying catalog houses as well. They are also safer for the tier, and some have replaceable blades. The choice is up to you. I got through years without ever using one; now I wouldn't be caught without one. It's simply a matter of personal preference.

HALF-HITCH TOOL: This is another handy little gadget designed to make finishing off the heads of the flies easier—especially with fine threads. It has a hole in the end of a taper, and the thread is wrapped around the tool, the hole placed over the eye of the hook, and the thread drawn off the tool onto the hook making a perfect half-hitch. The end of a peacock quill can be used, but the tool itself is so inexpensive (about fifty cents) that it is hardly worth improvising.

Incidentally, you will see whip finishers advertised for making smoother, more durable heads. If, instead of making two turns of thread on the half-hitch tool, you make six before transferring the thread to the hook, you will find you have an excellent substitute for a whip finish—a smooth head, with the end of the thread buried under five turns of thread. Very pretty, and very strong—and much simpler than a whip finish.

BODKIN: Not to be confused with a bobbin, the bodkin is a needle in a handle used for picking out fur bodies, releasing trapped filaments

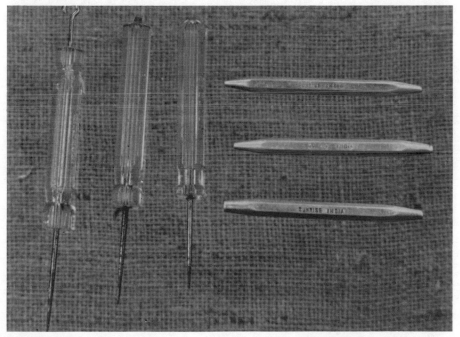

Bodkins   Half-Hitch Tools

21

of hackle, transferring head cement to the fly head, and a multitude of other uses. They can be purchased for anywhere from 35¢ to $1.50, or you can make a few by shoving the eye of a needle into a balsa-wood handle. They come in handy, whatever they look like.

That's about it for the required tools; obviously, to anyone who has had occasion to look at the flytiers' "wish books," there are a great number of other tools you can buy if you so desire: whip finishers, tool stands, tweezers, wing formers, magnifying glasses, hook snellers, winging pliers, mirrors, jeweler's loupes for examining the flies, hackle guards, hackle gauges, material clips, and on and on. By all means, add whatever you want; however, for the flies used in this book, only the above-mentioned tools are required, and as already stated, you can get by without the bobbin, the half-hitch tool, the scalpel, and

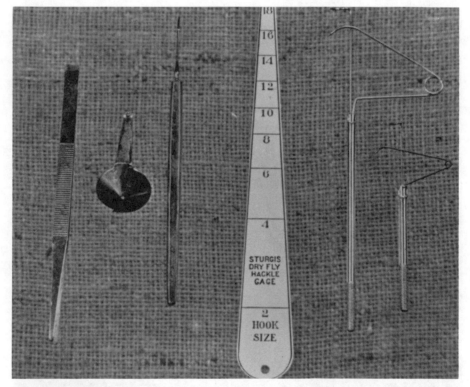

Miscellaneous Tools
(left to right)
Tweezers
Hackle Guard
Scalpel
Sturgis Hackle Gauge
Large Whip Finisher
Small Whip Finisher

the bodkin if you absolutely have to. But when you consider that the cost of the bodkin, scalpel, and half-hitch tool will not run over $2.00 (far less if you use a single-edged razor blade), they really are a wise investment.

Incidentally, if you happen to know a high-school or college teacher, ask him to get you a small dissecting kit through the school. It will cost about two dollars, but in it you will get a scalpel, a pair of heavy-duty scissors, and two or more bodkins—a good price any way you look at it, considering it comes in its own storage case, and the quality of the tools is excellent. With the tools at hand, now it's time to take a look at the sorts of materials you will be needing for tying the terrestrials.

MATERIALS

Flytiers collect an inordinate amount of materials—feathers, fur, hair, and other miscellany—from all variety of creatures that walk and fly. But for the purposes of tying the four dozen patterns covered by this book, we can limit the variety a certain amount. Then, as you progress into other patterns, you will be able to add whatever is required for those patterns, and you will have the skill and experience to judge more properly what is actually needed than you would have if suddenly faced by a materials catalog with its tremendous variety of different materials, some of which are used on no more than one or two patterns of fly.

FURS: First and foremost in tying the terrestrials is fur, which is used to make the bodies on many of the patterns offered in the later chapters. Fur has a certain translucency in the water that resembles an insect's body, and the texture is soft enough so that the fish may hold onto the fly that extra fraction of a second which means the difference between a missed strike and a hooked fish. There are several types of furs commonly used in fly tying, all of which can be used for tying the terrestrials. Some of the more notable are as follows:

Rabbit: Perhaps the most common of all fly-tying furs, rabbit is available from all the fly materials houses, in both natural and dyed colors. It is soft, translucent in the water, spins on the tying thread easily, and, most important, blends readily with other furs to achieve special colors. Rabbit has the added advantage of being inexpensive, but it does absorb water readily, making it effective mainly for wet flies rather than dries.

Muskrat: Next to the rabbit, muskrat is the most important fur for the flytier; I would go so far as to say that, with rabbit and muskrat fur in a wide range of colors, the tier could imitate just about any

23

fur body required. Muskrats, being water animals, have natural oils to their fur that give an excellent translucency in the water, and have a tendency to float better as well when treated with dry fly spray, since they don't absorb water as readily. Again, muskrat fur is readily available from all catalog houses.

Mink: Mink has recently come into its own as a fly-tying fur, for several reasons. First, the natural oils in the fur are superior to even those of the muskrat. Secondly, dying removes some of those oils, but since mink are pen-raised in a wide variety of colors, the different shades of pen-raised mink come to the flytier with all of their natural oils still intact. Mink is available both in body pieces and tails, and the tails are the best bet. The guard hairs on the tails are excellent for tails on some of the smaller flies (thrips, leaf hoppers, etc.) and the underfur provides excellent dubbing material. Mink tails cost approximately a dollar apiece, but each tail will provide enough guard hairs to tail several hundred flies, and enough dubbing material to create at least a gross of fly bodies, and they are actually quite economical.

Beaver: Like muskrat, beaver is a staple of the flytier's craft. Beaver comes in natural brown and ginger, and everything I have said about the muskrat fur applies to that of the beaver, and more. Beaver is more expensive, and can be done without, but on special patterns it does a superior job.

Seal: Seal fur comes in many colors, both natural and dyed. It is exceptionally translucent in the water, but because of the short nature of the individual hairs, it is difficult to spin onto the thread. I personally will not use seal anymore due to the manner in which baby seals are still being killed to provide the pelts for fur coats; as flytiers, we only get the leftovers, but even so, the sort of cruelty being displayed by the seal hunters to newborn animals that cannot defend themselves has no place in a supposedly civilized society such as ours, and I personally cannot condone it.

In addition to the above, there are many other natural furs, such as woodchuck, squirrel, fox, and the like, that have relatively limited applications for our purposes. Add them only if you want to experiment with other patterns.

Poly-X: Here is a material that will change your minds about furs. Would you believe a material with a density of less than water, in a color range that surpasses even dyed furs, offers greater translucency than the dyed furs and equal to the natural furs, and is easier to work with than furs? This man-made fiber does it all, and beautifully so. It can be purchased from Fly Fisherman's Bookcase and Rod and

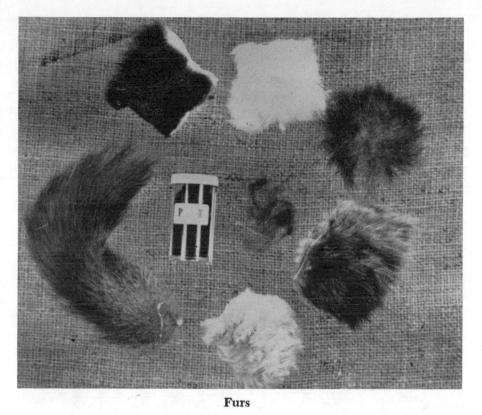

Furs

Otter	Bleached Beaver	Australian Opossum
Mink Tail	Poly-X	Muskrat
	Dyed Rabbit	

Reel among others, and a fifty-cent tube of the stuff will provide bodies for several hundred flies. By all means give it a try—you may never use fur bodies again. And even if the color range (over fifty colors available in all) isn't great enough, you can blend colors with the Poly-X even more readily than you can blend furs, and without anywhere near the mess. Also, it stores much more neatly than furs.

HAIR: The difference between furs and hair is that the hair is coarse, and used for wings and feelers, although some is used for the body as in the case of the cockroach, some of the grasshoppers, and a few others.

Deer Hair: Another flytier's staple, deer hair comes in a full range of colors. A hollow hair, it flares around the hook when thread is pulled tight against it. It is used for making the heads on the Muddler Minnow, head and wings on the Letort creations, and in a wide variety of other applications throughout the book. Obtain natural, black, and white, and a small piece of green. They are all you'll need. Caribou,

Hair

Porcupine
Woodchuck Tail   Horse Tail   Moose Mane
Calf Tail   Peccary
Deer Hair   Bucktail

antelope, and reindeer and elk hair have the same qualities, but are not as readily available, especially in colors.

Bucktail: The deer's tail is especially effective in winging certain of the patterns in this book. The hair of the tails is not hollow, and therefore does not flare as dramatically. The colors required are the same as mentioned for deer hair.

Moose Mane: This is a long, coarse hair, ranging in color from white to almost black (in the same piece). It is used primarily in making feelers, and can be effectively used as legs on some insects. It knots well, so that the joints of the legs of certain insects can be simulated. However, after knotting the moose mane, apply a drop of rubber cement to the knot to strengthen it in case it later becomes brittle.

Peccary: Peccary or javelina is a small Southwestern pig with very stiff bristles, light brown to cream in color. The individual hairs make excellent antennae, legs, and ovipositors (see section on characteristics of terrestrials). This hair is available in packages, and is well worth its small cost.

Horsehair: This is the hair from the tail of the horse, and is used primarily to make woven bodies. When two colors are woven together they make a very natural-looking body, especially if a lighter shade of the color is woven as the belly of the insect. Horsehair can be obtained in brown, black, golden, and white, and it would not be amiss to have on hand a packet of each color, since it is quite inexpensive.

MISCELLANEOUS BODY MATERIALS: Certain other materials are used from time to time in making bodies for the terrestrials. Briefly, they are as follows:

Kapok: Kapok is a plant fiber with superior floating characteristics; it's the same material that's used in life preservers, so you can guess

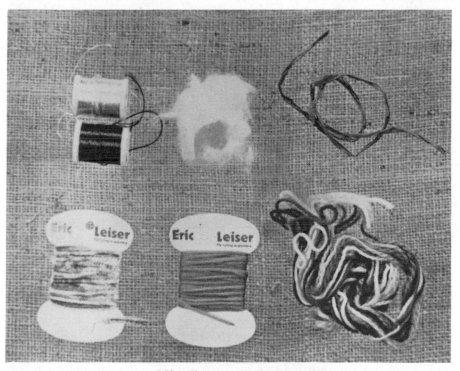

Miscellanous Body Materials

Floss	Kapok	Raffia
Chenille	Poly Yarn	Wool

how well it floats. It is a natural cream shade, but it can be dyed. It is very inexpensive, and good to have around.

Raffia: Raffia is another plant material, this time an African grass. It comes in various colors and is used to wrap fly bodies, providing a segmented appearance. It must be soaked before using.

Floss: The old-time flytier's standby, regular floss is not used for the terrestrials. However, acetate floss is used in red, tan, and black to make the hardshell ants. When dipped into a solvent solution (acetone) the wrapped body softens, and then solidifies upon contact with the air, making a hard, plasticlike body. Ant imitations tied with this acetate floss have the precise appearance and texture of living ants.

Wool: Wool is used in a few patterns where bulky bodies are required and translucency and floating qualities are not. If there aren't some old scraps in gray, white, green, and brown lying around the house, then purchase the smallest quantity you can, and only as you need it. Wool bodies have come into disrepute in recent years among flytiers, and while this attitude is not completely justified, there are so many better body materials available that you won't be using much of it.

Chenille: Chenille, which consists of small fibers twisted between two threads, is used occasionally in the same colors listed for wool to create a bulky, fuzzy body. Add the colors black and yellow, and you will be able to tie the woolly worm patterns to great effect.

FEATHERS: Feathers are highly important for various operations in tying the terrestrials. Rather than going into them fully here, I will briefly mention the most commonly used feathers, their general appearance, and the uses to which they are put in the patterns we shall be tying.

Wing Quills: From either ducks or geese, wing quills come in a wide range of colors, the most useful being brown, gray, black, and white. The fibers are used for making wings on flies, and wing cases or shells on the beetles, sowbugs, and the like. The tips of the quills themselves, round, hard, and in various colors, are used for making extension bodies for the grasshoppers, wasps, and walking sticks.

Turkey: The wing feathers from the turkey, in brown, bronze, and cinnamon, are used for the same purposes as those from the ducks and geese, but the mottled effect of the turkey wing makes it a much more natural choice on all the hoppers, and many of the other patterns as well. Have several matched pairs on hand, since this is one of the most important feathers used in this book.

Turkey Feathers

Striped Primary   White-Tipped Tail   Mottled Brown

Pheasant: All of the feathers of the ring-necked pheasant are useful to the flytier, especially to the tier of terrestrials. Some of them can be substituted for turkey feathers; the fibers of the tail are excellent for legs, antennae, and ribbing; the shoulder and breast feathers make excellent wing cases and shells for the beetles (especially the June bug) ; in short, the uses of the pheasant are virtually unlimited. You can purchase a whole skin for about $2.50—and you'll end up using the whole thing.

Mallard: The breast and side feathers, with their light brown bars on a white to cream background, are highly effective as wings on the thrips, the flying ants, and some of the landflies.

Peacock herl: This is a fuzzy, metallic green or bronze fiber from the tail feather of the peacock, used to wind butts and heads on some patterns, for ribbing on others, and as legs and feelers. It is inexpensive, and well worth having.

Mallard Wings Complete
Light Gray Paired Quills

Starling: The small, black breast and shoulder feathers from the starling, when lacquered, make superb wings and wing cases for the jassids and the smaller beetles; the white-tipped feathers are excellent for wings on ants and a few others.

HACKLES

Because of the importance of hackles to fly tying in general, I have set hackle necks apart from the other feathers; and I do mean hackle necks. You will need five for the patterns in this book, and with the exception of the grizzly they are relatively inexpensive—never purchase loose hackles in packages. The neck is the only way of being assured of a full range of sizes, and purchasing the necks from a reputable dealer is the only way of being assured of getting decent quality. Unless you really know what to look for in a neck cape, tell the dealer what you want it for and trust him; he won't do you wrong, for the simple reason that he wants your business again.

The five colors of necks needed for the terrestrials, along with their descriptions, are as follows:

MEDIUM DUN: A light blue-gray. This will have to be a dyed neck, since natural necks of this shade are so scarce as to be almost non-

Hackle Necks

Brown		Ginger
	Grizzly	
Blue Dun		Badger

31

existent. Order one dyed by the Eric Leiser Photo dyeing process—Rod and Reel and Fly Fisherman's Bookcase both supply this sort, and it is a far superior method of obtaining the color than any other sort of dyeing.

BROWN: Just what the name implies; a rich brown color with just a hint of a reddish touch. A natural color, quite common, and relatively inexpensive.

GINGER: This is a buff or sand-colored hackle, with a slight hint of red, sometimes so pale as to be almost impossible to see. This neck, the brown, and the dun, will be the most often-used necks in tying the terrestrials.

BADGER: The badger is a pale, creamy color with a black stripe running down the center. When wound on the hook, the badger hackle provides a black center surrounded by a creamy halo—very much like the beating wings of some insects. It is also used in tying spent wing thrips.

GRIZZLY: The most expensive of the necks, because it is one of the scarcest. It comes from the Plymouth Rock rooster, and is of a very dark gray with white bars. However, it is one of the most effective colors for simulating insect wings and legs that exists, and the flytier without at least one good grizzly cape will not be able to tie the most effective patterns.

WAX

All thread should be waxed; either purchase prewaxed thread or, if you are going to eliminate the use of a bobbin, purchase a cake of fly-tying wax and wax each section of thread separately. Waxing strengthens the thread, makes it lay better, and is absolutely essential when spinning a dubbed body.

THREAD

Whether you choose silk or nylon, purchase a good quality thread from the catalog houses in black, white, gray, and orange.

HOOKS

The subject of hooks is so involved that it need not be dealt with here; there are many excellent books on the subject should you be interested. For each pattern in the book, the proper style and size of hook will be given at the beginning of the instructions. Use that style of hook, and you won't go wrong.

And now, on to the terrestrials.

3
CHARACTERISTICS OF TERRESTRIALS

If the flytier is to be able to properly construct effective imitations of the terrestrials (or any other flies for that matter), it is necessary for him to have at least a basic understanding of the external physical characteristics of insects, so that these may be taken into consideration in the imitations of the naturals. Since this book, however, is not designed to be a course in entomology, the description of the insect characteristics will be rather limited, simply to provide a general understanding of the various parts of the insects, and how most patterns should be constructed to most properly duplicate the living insects. The appendix dealing with collecting and preserving the naturals will also include a list of selected references, dealing with both collecting and with studying entomology as well, so that the interested flytier can pursue his study further.

In general the body of any insect is rather elongated, and consists of various segments, which are divided into three primary sections known as the head, the thorax, and the abdomen. The appendages that are attached to these three general sections are located in the following manner: eyes, sensory antennae, and mouth parts on the head; legs and wings on the thorax; and reproductive appendages at the rear end of the abdomen. The insects are invertebrates—that is, they possess no internal skeletal structure—rather the supportive mechanism is called an exoskeleton, or hardening of the integument, which is known technically as sclerotization; and, in turn, the various segments and plates on the surface of the insect's body are termed sclerites.

The head of the insect is usually rather small in proportion to the rest of the body, and much harder than the abdomen. There are generally several plates on the head, each of which bears a particularized name. Most insects as well bear two types of eyes—usually three simple eyes known as ocelli, although the number may vary or the ocelli be nonexistent in some species; and two compound eyes that are composed of many facets. The ocelli, where present, are located on the frontal plane of the head, while the compound eyes are located dorsolaterally, the latter generally taking up most of the space on the head.

The antennae are important for duplication of the naturals, and length should be taken into consideration, since in the natural insects the antennae, composed of different numbers of segments, are frequently used to distinguish among different groups of insects. The antennae generally project forward from the middle of the head, just below the ocelli—very seldom from the top of the head as has been the general rule in imitations to date. The mouth parts of the insects are not of great importance to the flytier, since they are among the fine details that cannot be effectively duplicated except in a few instances—such as the landflies—where the mouth parts are rather pendulous and designed for sucking. These can generally be duplicated to advantage with the tip of a hackle quill tied in to extend beneath the head and a bit forward; we shall discuss that at greater length in the chapter dealing with the landflies.

The thorax, for the flytier, is the most important part of the imitation. It is from the thorax that all of the locomotor appendages originate—legs and wings. There are three segments to the thorax, termed the prothorax, the mesothorax, and the metathorax. Each of these segments typically carries a pair of legs, extending laterally from the ventral, or lower, side of the thorax; and the mesothorax and metathorax produce the wings, extending laterally from the dorsal, or top side of the thorax, but hinged in most cases in the terrestrials so that they can be laid flat along the dorsum of the thorax and abdomen.

Each segment of the thorax consists of four groups of sclerites, known as the notum on the dorsal side, a pair of pleura in the sides (laterally) and the sternum beneath, or ventrally. By using the prefix of the thoracic segments applied to the sclerites, enthomologists can determine exactly which sclerite is being referred to—for example, the metapleura would be recognized immediately as the lateral sclerites of the metathoracic segment. The further divisions of these sclerites is quite interesting to the streamside entomologist, but since the minute scutum, scutellum, postnotum, mesoscutellum, pleural sutures, episternum, and epimeron are not readily duplicated on artificial flies, particularly on sizes #12 and smaller, there is no need to cover them in a chapter of a book such as this.

The legs of the terrestrials, however, are of importance since, especially in the larger types of insects, such as the walkingsticks, the cockroaches, the grasshoppers, and the crickets, the legs are a very evident part of the insect, and play an important role in fooling the fish into believing that the creation above it is an actual insect. The legs of insects generally contain the following parts: the coxa, which is the basal segment of the leg originating from the body; the trochanter, which is a small juncture between the coxa and the femur; the femur itself, corresponding to the thigh in man (the most dramatic example is the femur of the grasshopper, tremendously developed for its muscular leaps); the tibia; and the tarsa, which are segments corresponding generically to the human foot, and ending generally in two tarsal claws and one or more tarsal pads. The legs vary tremendously from insect to insect, and so description of the individual requirements for each of the artificials will be given in their respective chapters.

There is also tremendous variation in insect wings, from the hairy wings of the thrips through the rather leathery membranes of the grasshoppers to the hard sheathed wings of the beetles. Again, individual wing requirements will be given as needed in the chapters pertaining to the individual insects.

Wing venation, or the structure of the veins in the wings of the insects, is a fascinating study in itself, but it has no bearing upon the flytier, since the tier is using materials to suggest the wings, which have no veins. Herter's puts out a veined wing material that is extremely effective in many patterns, but even in a case such as that the venation of the plastic material is standard and cannot be varied to actually dupicate the actual wings of the different insects. The flytier

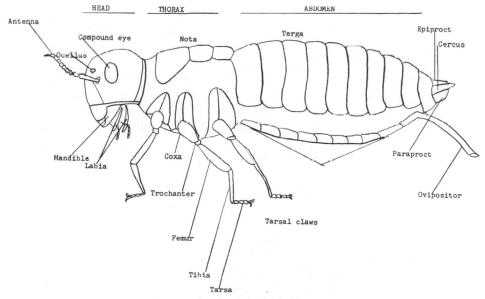

Insect Anatomy Simplified

has to draw the line somewhere in imitations, and wing venation is one place where this line must be drawn. In any event, it is extremely doubtful as to whether or not the venation of the wings has anything to do with fish-taking ability, for the simple reason that when most of the winged terrestrials fall on the water their wings are either furled beneath the cases or upright. In the cases of the insects such as the thrips and landflies, which may land in a spent position, hackle feather tips, especially dun or grizzly, simulate general translucent venation more than adequately for the flytier's purposes.

Finally, the abdomen of the insects generally contains eleven segments, although a certain amount of fusing may cause fewer, and the eleventh, or tail segment, is generally small and contains the reproductive organs. These need not be covered in detail, due to the fact that most of the time they are drawn into the body cavity. For an identification of these various parts, see the illustration of the eleventh segment. The one appendage that is important to the flytier is present on the females of certain species, and is known as the ovipositor. This is the egg-laying appendage, and stems from modification of structures found on the eighth and ninth abdominal segments. It is a rather long tube that extends past the tip of the abdomen, and that is inserted in soil or rotten wood, among other things, in order to deposit the eggs produced by the female. In many insects the ovipositor is always external; in some it can be withdrawn into the body when not in use.

I'm not recommending that you study insect anatomy with an eye to duplicating every characteristic of the living insect on your artificials, for the simple reason that it cannot be done. In fact, in most instances, we can only approximate a characteristic. But it is the approximation of those characteristics which are left off so many of the commercially tied flies that can mean the difference between an ignored offering and a smashing strike.

However, it still goes without saying that you at least have to know a little about what you are trying to duplicate in order to do it effectively. A grasshopper with black wings will not catch the fish that a grasshopper with mottled wings will fool, for the simple reason that almost all grasshoppers have mottled wings, and the fish are used to seeing them that way. In the same light, a perfectly tied thrip on a #8 hook won't fool a single fish in low water, for the simple reason that thrips grow no larger than a size #20.

For the angler who wishes to go further with his studies, I refer him to the entomological books in the appendix. The terrestrials are, if anything, more interesting than the water insects that have made up the bulk of the fly-fisherman's repertoire for so many decades—they are easier to capture, easier to preserve and study, and far easier to raise in captivity. Now it's time to take a look at some of the individual insects, their specific characteristics, and how to tie their imitations.

4

GRASSHOPPERS

Grasshoppers were the first insects that got me interested in terrestrials as a major element of fly-fishing, in 1974. I was fishing a small meadow stream on Maryland's Eastern Shore, near Denton, a stream that was known not only for huge bluegills but also for occasional bass in the one- to two-pound category, and I had been on the stream for three hours without so much as a strike. I would have thought that the stream was barren if it hadn't been for the maddening fact that fish were constantly slurping the water in the tall grasses that overhung the stream's margins.

I had tried practically everything in my fly boxes, including a Muddler Minnow to attempt an imitation of the small sculpins that frequented the bottom. I was fishing the Muddler at the time, and becoming more and more upset with every futile cast. Then one of

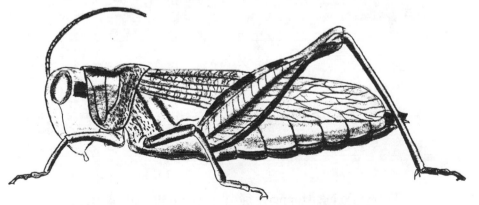

Common Short Horned Grasshopper

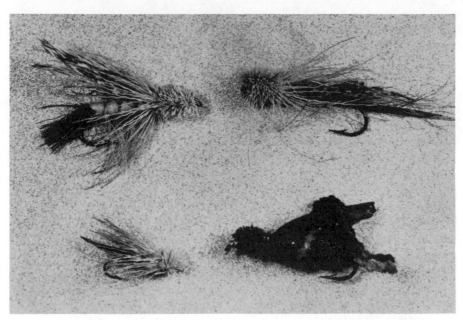

Dave's Hopper   Muddler Minnow
Letort Hopper   Deer Hair Hopper

Turkey Wing Hopper   Quill-Bodied Hopper
Wilson Hopper   Michigan Hopper

my casts was caught by a light gust of wind, and the Muddler dropped astraddle a frond of grass that was floating down the stream. I was just about to twitch it off the grass blade when a V-wake rushed from the nearby shore grasses and engulfed both grass and fly, and I was into a nice stream largemouth.

I was wondering why the Muddler had elicited such a dramatic attack so suddenly after all the futile casts, and after I had released the fish I started poking around in the streamside grasses. The answer became immediately apparent. The grass was full of grasshoppers close to the edge of the stream, although for some reason they had not been prevalent farther back on land. At any rate, it was obvious that with such a feast at hand, the fish in that stream were not about to bother with anything but hoppers. I chose a slightly smaller Muddler, a #10, and coated it heavily with dry-fly spray, and within the next two hours I had caught and released over sixteen nice fish, including a two-pound largemouth and a seventeen-ounce bluegill.

There is no such thing as a complete selection of grasshopper imitations, due to the fact that there are approximately ten thousand species known in the world, and of those about six hundred species are inhabitants of the continental United States. Technically, they are leaping insects belonging to the insect order Orthoptera, in the families Acrididae and Tettigoniidae. Their habitat is virtually universal, and they are found in mountains and marshes, deserts and meadows. They are especially prevalent in fields and along roadsides from midsummer through early fall, and in general are colored in varying shades of brown, olive, and green, although many of the foreign species and a few of the American species are rather garishly colored.

Long before politics entered the realm of man's worries, mankind had waged a dreadful war against members of the grasshopper family. They caused one of the plagues of Egypt, and every schoolboy is familiar with the tale of the locust plague upon the Mormon settlers under Brigham Young at Salt Lake City. Grasshoppers are entirely herbivorous, meaning that they eat only plant material, with some species limited to specific plants, and when massive swarms of migratory locusts start to move, they can strip the vegetation from everything in sight in a very short time. Luckily, only a very few species are this economically detrimental; it is questionable as to whether or not mankind could survive if all ten thousand species were such severe destroyers of crops.

The characteristic sound of the grasshoppers is caused by rubbing the toothed inner edge of the greatly enlarged femurs against a raised vein on the wings.

For the purposes of the flytier, the grasshoppers of greatest importance are the short-horned grasshoppers of the family Acrididae. They are called short-horned grasshoppers because the antennae are rather

39

short in proportion to the body and heavy. The Acrididae females have well-developed ovipositors, and it doesn't hurt to have a few patterns with the ovipositor in evidence. In size, grasshoppers range from less than an inch in length (Pygmy grasshopper, family Tetrigidae) to almost two inches (Spurthroated grasshoppers, subfamily Cyrtacanthaccridinae; Slant-faced grasshoppers, subfamily Acridinae; and Band-winged grasshoppers, subfamily Oedipodinae). The following patterns, tied in sizes #4 to #12, in shades of brown, cinnamon, and olive, will effectively cover most of the species found throughout the United States; some of the Western species are larger, and in some cases the grasshoppers may be of a more yellow hue, and if none of the patterns given in the following pages are as effective as you feel they should be, try capturing a live hopper from the area in which you fish, and tie the same patterns substituting materials that more nearly approximate the local coloration. However, I have fished over a good part of the best waters, and I have seldom had at least one of the patterns fail to produce.

THE LETORT HOPPER

The original Letort Hopper, like the Letort Cricket in the next chapter, was developed by Ed Shenk, and there are few hopper patterns that are more effective. The original dressing is as follows:

Hook: #'s 10, 12, regular of 2X long (Mustad #94842 or #9671).
Thread: Yellow or brown.
Abdomen: Mixture of olive, tan, and yellow Poly-X or rabbit fur dubbing.
Thorax: Same as abdomen.
Underwing: Brown mottled turkey wing section, cut in one piece and folded downwing over thorax and abdomen.
Wing: Natural deer hair tied over turkey quill section and slightly flared.
Head: The butts of the deer hair wing flared fully and kept on top of the hook. Trimmed to shape.

First, affix the hook in the vise and start the thread one third of the way back from the eye, and wrap smoothly to a point where the bend of the hook begins. Half-hitch the thread at this point, and add additional wax to the thread. Now blend the Poly-X or rabbit fur to an even shade, and spin it onto the waxed section of thread by twisting the thread and body material together, in *one direction only*, until the body material is securely affixed to the length of thread. Now wind the body material onto the hook shank in close, heavy turns to give the appearance of segmentations, and tie it off 1/8" behind the eye.

Now cut a section of turkey wing quill, ⅜″ in width, coat it with rubber cement, and allow it to dry. The rubber cement will reinforce the fibers of the underwing, and will keep the fly in good shape through several strikes. When the rubber cement has dried, fold the section of wing quill in half and trim it as shown in the illustration. Tie it on top of the hook so that it lies flat on top of the dubbing, extending to the end of the body, and slightly overlapping the sides. Trim off the surplus feather extending over the eye of the hook.

Now cut a small bunch of natural deer hair, pinch it tightly between your left thumb and forefinger, and hold it on top of the hook so that the tips extend to the end of the turkey feather and the butts overlap the eye. Pull the thread over the top of the deer hair and down, causing the butts to flare—but make certain that you keep the deer hair pinched tightly on top of the hook. If you let go the deer hair will flare all the way around the hook and you'll have to start over again. Wrap several times, crisscrossing the thread through the butts of the deer hair to get a full, even flare, and tie off just behind the eye.

Now trim the deer hair butts to a nicely rounded head, and apply some thin lacquer to the thread, so that it soaks into the base of the head. This will reinforce the head of the fly, while still allowing the flared deer hair to perform its function. Trim off the surplus thread with a razor blade, and the Letort Hopper is complete.

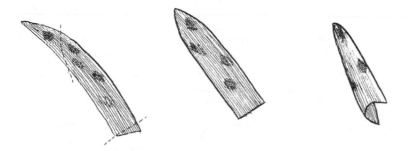

Cut Wing Slip
Trimmed
Folded and ready for application to fly body

MICHIGAN HOPPER

The Michigan Hopper has proved to be an effective fly when small grasshoppers are on the water. Bill Blades, the master flytier, tied this number with a tail of red hackle fibers for a reason that I could never understand (Ray Bergman's book, *Trout,* also lists a hopper pattern similar to this one with a red hackle fiber tail), since

I have never seen a grasshopper with a tail, red or otherwise. I generally leave off the tail, but I will present the pattern in its original form for the hard-bound traditionalists. If it doesn't come up to your expectations, simply clip the tail off, and I believe you will find that its effectiveness will be improved.

Hook: #'s 12, 14, 2X long (Mustad #9671).
Body: Yellow wool, extending over bend of hook.
Tail: Red hackle fibers.
Wings: Brown mottled turkey.
Hackle: Brown and grizzly mixed, palmered lightly, and heavy at head.
Thread: Black.

Tie on the thread as you did for the Letort Hopper, and, at the bend of the hook, tie in six to eight red hackle fibers, extending the length of the hook bend past the hook. Now double a loop of medium-heavy yellow wool, and tie it in so that the loop extends past the bend of the hook ¾ the length of the tail fibers. At this point, tie in a brown and a grizzly hackle feather, each moderately long.

Advance the thread to ⅛" behind the eye of the hook, and wrap the wool forward and tie it off at that point. Now grip the butts of the two hackles with the hackle pliers and spiral them forward evenly (about four turns). Tie them off, but do not cut off the surplus yet.

Prepare a section of turkey wing quill in the same manner as that for the Letort Hopper, and tie it in behind the surplus hackle, trimming the palmer hackle at the top and sides so that the wing quill lies over the body like a tent. Now finish winding the hackle at the head into a fairly bushy collar, tie it off, trim off the surplus, and make a neat, small head of thread and lacquer it.

The Michigan Hopper, with its woolen body, is very difficult to keep afloat, so don't bother. Simply fish it on a dead drift under overhanging grasses and banks. In the early season when the hoppers are small it can be deadly.

QUILL-BODIED HOPPER

The Quill-Bodied Hopper is a pattern originated by Doug Swisher and Carl Richards. I have used it on occasion, and I must say that it is extremely effective. However, it is rather difficult to tie, and has the added problem of coming apart after one or two good strikes. If you want to make up a few, I would suggest that you save them for the big lunker under the bank who won't take anything else. At least then the destroyed fly will be worth the tying of another.

I tie the Quill-Bodied Hopper slightly differently than do Swisher and Richards, since my method makes the fly a bit simpler and more durable.

Hook: #'s 6–10, 3X long (Mustad #9672).
Body: Goose wing quill tip, 1½x the length of the hook, and covered with yellow or olive Mohlon (synthetic spun fur) or chenille.
Wing: Brown mottled turkey.
Legs: Small turkey quills.
Thread: Brown or olive.

Begin by cutting a small hole on the goose quill tip halfway back from the end. Insert the eye of the hook into this hole and run it through so that the eye extends approximately ⅛" from the open end of the quill. Now, keeping the hook shank in the center of the quill, fill the quill with Duco cement and allow the cement to dry while suspending the hook from a wire. Since a small portion of the bend will be inside the quill when it is filled, once the cement has hardened the body should not turn on the hook shank.

After the cement is thoroughly dry, tie in a length of Mohlon at the head of the fly, directly in front of the quill body, and wrap it all the way to the quill tip and back again. In order to get the Mohlon to remain on the rounded hackle tip (if it slips off, you'll have one devil of a mess) coat the last half inch of the quill tip *thinly* with Duco cement, allow the cement to get tacky, and wrap the Mohlon through it. Admittedly, this will cause a very slight discoloration of the Mohlon in this area, but since most grasshoppers are mottled, anyway, the discoloration may serve to enhance the fly's attractiveness—at any rate, it certainly doesn't detract from it. When the Mohlon reaches the head of the fly again, form an even taper between the abrupt end of the quill and the hook shank. Tie off the Mohlon, and trim off the surplus.

Once again, prepare a section of turkey feather in the manner used for the preceding hoppers, and tie it on top of the Mohlon-covered quill, using thread of the same color as the Mohlon so that the juncture appears as the segmentation between the head and the thorax, with the butt of the wing approximately ⅜" back from the end of the quill and the tip extending slightly past the end of the quill. Bind the butt down thoroughly so that no excess quill extends past the bindings.

Up until this point the fly will be quite durable, but now you will be installing the legs made from turkey quill tips, and these are the first to go in a strike. Clip the ends off two small turkey quills, making the sections about ½" in length. You will notice that the turkey quill tips are solid, that is, they are filled with pith. With a single-edged razor blade or a surgeon's scalpel, shave away a 3/16" section on the side of the quill to the squared-off end, taking away half the diameter

43

of the quill for that length, and leaving a flat area on the quill tip. Do this with both sections. It is imperative that you have the greatest amount of surface area available on these flats for the next operation.

Now take your Duco cement again, and thoroughly saturate a strip as wide as the quill sections on the body of the hopper, on both sides, $\frac{1}{3}$ of the way back from the eye of the hook. Allow this cement to dry. The purpose in doing this is to create a nonporous surface, since the fly would be even less durable if you attempted to glue the legs directly to the fuzzy Mohlon. When the cement is almost set, either squeeze the body lightly with a pair of flat-jawed pliers, or press something flat and smooth against the glue on either side to form a flat surface. Allow the glue to dry thoroughly.

Now apply cement to the flattened sections of the quill legs, press them against the previously glued section of the body sloping backwards at a 45° angle, and clamp in place overnight with a spring-type clothespin.

As I have said, the first or second strike is going to break these legs off, and there is no way of applying them in a stronger manner that would be as effective to the final appearance of the fly. However, if the rest of the fly has been constructed in the prescribed manner, you can salvage the body and wings, and simply replace the kicker legs when necessary. Obviously, with the tremendous amount of time involved in tying the quill-bodied hopper, you won't want to use it indiscriminately. Wait for the big 'un that won't take any other offering, then blast him with this fly and say to hell with the legs.

TURKEY WING HOPPER

Turkey Wing Hopper is a rather simple name for a creation, since all hoppers that are effective have wings made of turkey wing sections. However, this is another Swisher-Richards pattern with a different type of kicking leg, and the silhouette is rather effective. I have found that when the fish are taking this hopper, however, they will take others as well, so I merely present this in its original form for your edification, and I introduce a new style of tying the legs. Certainly it is more durable than the Quill-Bodied Hopper, if not as dramatically effective.

Hook: #'s 6 to 12, 2X long (Mustad #9671).
Body: Yellow Mohlon, extended or looped beyond bend of hook.
Wings: Brown mottled turkey feather section.
Legs: Pheasant tail fibers or bronze peacock herl, knotted and
    looped.

Make the body of Mohlon in the same way you made the woolen body for the Michigan Hopper, with a loop extending past the bend of the hook, and tie on the wing section in the standard manner. Now take several peacock herls, or the longest pheasant tail fibers you can find, knot them together in the middle, bring the tips down to the butts, and tie them together onto the fly ⅓ of the way back from the head. Do this on both sides.

If the legs are tied on after the wing is tied down, there will be an extra bond on the wing, and this will make the fly more durable. You may, if you wish, tie the legs on before affixing the wing, which will avoid the small band of thread on the top and sides of the wing itself.

In the Swisher-Richards original, the wing is allowed to extend forward over the head, so traditionalists may proceed in that manner. Personally, I have never seen a living grasshopper constructed in that manner, so I tie the pattern so that the wings originate approximately ¼″ in front of the legs. The choice is up to you.

DEER HAIR HOPPER

The Deer Hair Hopper is an excellent exercise in creative barbering, since the body is formed of spun deer hair clipped into a hopper shape. In the Swisher-Richards book, *Selective Trout,* they describe a Deer Hair Hopper that is very impressionistic, having a wing made of flared deer hair. I am afraid that I have little faith in that pattern, since hoppers are so prevalent and trout can easily recognize the shape of a hopper. The Swisher-Richards deer hair pattern looks a little more like an embryonic bat, so if the fish in your neighborhood are in the habit of feeding on embryonic bats, by all means purchase a copy of their excellent book (seriously, their concept of No-Hackle flies is one of the best developments in the art of fly tying and fishing in a long while) and try the pattern.

My version of the Deer Hair Hopper is slightly more realistic, and I have had excellent success with it, particularly in fast-flowing meadow streams, where the hollow deer hair keeps the fly floating high and dry much longer than any other pattern.

Hook: #s 8 to 12, 6X long (Mustad #3665A).
Body: Yellow, green, or olive deer hair spun on hook shank and clipped to shape.
Wing: Turkey wing quill sections.
Kicking legs: Green dyed chenille pipe cleaner.
Thread: 3/0 white nylon.

Start the thread at a point directly opposite the barb of the hook. Do *not* wrap the entire shank, because if you do the deer hair will not spin properly. Now, take a rather hefty pinch of deer hair, grasp it between your thumb and forefinger, and lay it on top of the hook above the barb. Take one turn of thread over the center of the bunch, and start pulling down. When the deer hair starts to flare, bring the thread up over the bunch again, and gently release your grip on the deer hair. It will follow the thread around the hook, flaring as it goes, and forming a perfect collar that will look quite a bit like a hair hackle. Take several turns of thread through the hair to make it flare fully, half-hitch the thread and apply a drop of rod varnish to the half-hitch.

Now add another bunch in a like manner, and after it has flared, shove it firmly back against the first bunch. Proceed in this manner to a distance of 1/8″ behind the eye of the hook, and tie off with several half-hitches. The rod varnish on each half-hitch will strengthen the tie, and will also strengthen the body of the fly.

What you now have looks a bit like a very small but angry cat. Clip off the excess thread and take the hook from the vise. Holding the hook by the bend, take your scissors and begin trimming the deer hair into the shape of a grasshopper. Go very slowly at first, because extra hair can always be clipped off, but if you cut too much you can't add it back on again. A slightly deeper clipping about 3/8″ back from the eye will give separation to the head.

Once the fly has been trimmed to shape, place it back in the vise, and work a short piece of tying thread down into the deer hair, 1/3 of the way back from the front of the head. Now take half a pipe cleaner that has been dyed green and work it into the deer hair from the bottom, bending it around the hook shank one full turn and tying it securely with several figure eights of thread. In this manner the pipe cleaner should not twist on the hook shank. In order to be absolutely certain, take a small bit of Duco cement on the point of your bodkin, and work it into the base of the deer hair around the pipe cleaner. The glue will bond the chenille to the deer hair when it is dry, and make the construction secure. Now take the ends of the pipe cleaner that extend out to the sides, bend them up and back at a 45° angle, then down at a 90° angle and finally bend the tarsa parallel to the shank.

The final step is to tie on the wings. Infiltrate the neck section (the groove between the head and body) with thinned head cement, and allow to harden. This provides a surface against which to tie the wing. Then bind on the turkey wing section, tie it off, and supply rod varnish to the windings. The rod varnish will make the white nylon thread almost transparent, and the fly is complete.

DAVE'S HOPPER

Dave's Hopper is a pattern originated by Dave Whitlock, a superb and creative Western flytier and fisherman. The Whitlock Hopper imitation is a complicated pattern, because it is, in effect, a synthesis of several patterns. Made in a wide variety of sizes, it nevertheless gives the appearance of great size, as do most of the patterns designed for fishing on the brawling Western streams. Nevertheless, it is a pattern that is equally effective in the rougher streams of the East, and also a superb pattern for bass waters throughout the country.

Hook: #s 6–14, 2X long (Mustad #9671).
Thread: Brown.
Tail: Brown deer hair, dyed red.
Body: Yellow wool.
Ribbing: One brown hackle, tied palmer.
Underwing: Yellow deer hair.
Wing: Brown mottled turkey.
Collar: Dun brown deer hair.
Head: Dun brown deer hair.

Start the thread one third of the way back from the eye, and wrap the rear ⅔ of the hook shank evenly. Take a small bunch of the dyed red deer hair and lay it on top of the hook so that the butts of the hair extend to the beginning of the thread wraps. Bind it down snugly, making sure that the hair stays on top of the hook in order to give depth to the finished body. Now apply a thin coat of head cement to give extra durability.

Now tie in the brown hackle opposite the barb of the hook, and tie in a strand of yellow wool, on top of the deer hair tail, and bind it down in the same manner as you did the tail hairs, adding still more height to the body. Make a loop on the wool, the same as in the case of the Michigan Hopper and the Turkey Wing Hopper, tie down the wool again, advance the tying thread to the beginning of the body section, spiral the wool forward, and tie it off. Now wrap the hackle forward in order to indicate a segmented body, wrapping it in the grooves formed by the wraps of the wool. Tie it off at the front of the body, and trim off the excess hackle and wool.

The underwing is made in the same manner that the overwing was made for the Letort Hopper, with the exception of the fact that the butts are not used to form the head, but rather are clipped off flush with the front of the body, still leaving the front ⅓ of the hook shank clear. The overwing is made from turkey wing feathers, as are the wings on all the hopper imitations. Whitlock uses two matched sections of turkey feather, tying in one on each side of the yellow deer hair underwing in standard wet fly fashion. There is no reason at all why the single piece cannot be used. Because of the underwing, however, it must be proportionately wider so that it will fit like a tent over the slightly flared deer hair.

The collar is now added with a small bunch of deer hair, flared in the manner used for the Deer Hair Hopper, and the head is formed in the same manner, keeping it close and tight. When making the collar, however, flare the hair closer to the butts so that the tips extend well out from the body. Then barber the head to the shape shown, allowing some of the longer collar hairs to extend out to the sides. They will serve to simulate legs, and also aid the hopper in floating in an upright position.

Apply a drop of head cement to the windings where the head was tied off, and Dave's Hopper is ready to go. It takes time to tie and, once again, I fail to see the reason for a tail on an imitation of an insect that has no tail, but I won't argue with success, because the Whitlock Hopper is indeed a very successful pattern.

WILSON'S HOPPER

This one is my own creation, designed primarily for those days in late summer when the water is so low and clear that you can see every beer can the picnickers have left in your favorite trout stream, and the fish can see every little detail of the flies you are presenting to them. As a result, this fly comes as close as is humanly possible to the actual configurations of a living hopper. A few of these in the box may save the day when the waters are low and clear, but it obviously is not a pattern that you would want to sit down and tie several dozen of.

Hook: #s 4–12, 6X long (Mustad #9575).
Thread: Black.
Body: Yellow, insect green, tan, or olive Poly-X.
Wing: Brown mottled turkey sections.
Kicking legs: Green dyed chenille pipe cleaner.
Walking legs: Pheasant breast feather.
Antennae: Two hairs from peccary.

Start the thread 1/16″ from the eye of the hook, and wrap the shank thoroughly to a point opposite the barb. Spin on a sizeable amount of Poly-X in the color of your choice. and wrap a full abdomen, half the length of the hook shank, and tapering abruptly at both ends to a cigar shape. Directly in front of the abdomen, tie in a length of green dyed chenille pipe cleaner in exactly the same manner as done for the Deer Hair Hopper, and bend them so that they extend upward and back at a 45° angle. Two-fifths of the way up the pipe cleaner, bend the wire and bring it back down at a 90° angle. Level with the spot at which it is tied to the hook shank, bend the pipe cleaner again, straight back this time, to simulate the tarsus. Do this on both sides. Now take a pheasant breast feather, and prepare it as shown in the drawing, so that the fibers are divided into two points on each side. Tie this to the bottom of the hook shank.

Now wrap the thorax, moderately heavy, letting the Poly-X separate the walking legs, so that they extend out of the body. This gives a

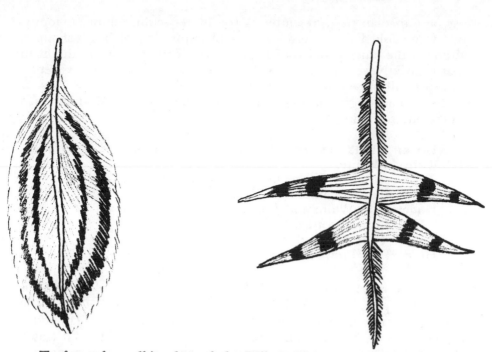

To form the walking legs of the Wilson Hopper, separate and stroke back the fibers of the pheasant body feather as shown, holding them together with lacquer or head cement. Allow to dry, trim other fibers as shown, and tie it in.

very natural-looking leg arrangement. Tie off the Poly-X and tie the wing section on top in the manner used for all the hopper imitations, allowing the wing to tent down almost to the legs, falling between the kicking legs.

In front of the thorax, tie in two pieces of peccary hair, one on either side of the hook, extending upward and forward past the eye of the hook at a 45° angle, and separate them with the tying thread so that they angle not only upward, but to the sides as well. Finish wrapping the Poly-X in the shape of the head, around and between the antennae, and tie it off neatly. Apply a drop of head cement to the knot, and the Wilson Hopper is complete. It takes time and trouble, but in late summer it is well worth the extra effort, and when properly tied the fly is quite durable. It possesses both the coloration *and* the silhouette of a real hopper, and short of providing artificial flavor you can't do much better when the fish are being really selective.

MUDDLER MINNOW

I can't really leave this section without a mention of the Muddler Minnow, since it was the fly that got me started on my study of the importance of terrestrials. The Muddler, created by Don Gapen for

49

use on Canadian trout, resembles a freshwater sculpin most obviously, but when fished dry it gives a passable imitation of a grasshopper, although the other patterns of hoppers have certainly superseded it in that regard. Nevertheless, it is still the best all-around fly in existence, and so I will present it here. By all means have a few of these in your boxes. No matter what the fish are feeding on, the Muddler is a marvelous searching fly.

> Hook: 1/0–12, 3X long (Mustad #9672, or Mustad #38941).
> Thread: White.
> Tail: Section of brown mottled turkey wing.
> Body: Flat gold tinsel.
> Underwing: White and brown calf tail, mixed.
> Wing: Brown mottled turkey.
> Collar: Dun brown deer hair.
> Head: Dun brown deer hair.

The Muddler Minnow is tied in basically the same manner as Dave's Hopper. The thread wraps the rear two thirds of the hook shank. Tie in a narrow section of brown mottled turkey feather for the tail, and at the same time tie in a length of medium gold tinsel. Wrap the thread back to the beginning, keeping the wraps jammed against each other to provide a smooth base for the tinsel. Now wrap the tinsel evenly forward, and tie it off, cutting or breaking off the surplus.

Now tie a small bunch of brown calf tail (about ten hairs) to the top of the hook shank, keeping them on top, and over these tie an equal bunch of white calf tail, still leaving the front third of the hook clear. On either side of the calf tail, tie a section of brown mottled turkey, each section taken from a matching wing quill so that they will be proportionate. The sections should curve inward and down at the tips, making a sort of tent but still allowing the white calf tail to peek through the top.

Now tie in the collar and the head of deer hair in precisely the same manner that you did for the Dave's Hopper. (I don't know for certain, but I would imagine that since Whitlock admits the pattern to be a synthesis of several other proven patterns, the style of the head and collar may well have come from the Muddler). Trim the head neatly, only with the Muddler allow the collar to extend all the way around the hook rather than simply out to the sides. Tie it off, and this most versatile fly is complete.

The grasshoppers make up a tremendous part of the terrestrial diet of various fish, and so they have been given a dominant position in the book. Whatever you do, don't let yourself be caught without at least a few of these patterns in your boxes. As you progress with your fishing you will find yourself switching to the terrestrials more and more when the other flies don't produce, and it wouldn't surprise me in the least if, after a year or so, your first cast just happens to be made with one of the hoppers.

5
CRICKETS

Crickets follow naturally upon the heels of the grasshoppers, because not only are they alike in general shape, but they are also of the same order of insects, Orthoptera. Of this order, the crickets make up the family Gryllidae, a family characterized by the musical chirping made by the males on warm nights, the rhythm of which bears a direct relationship to the temperature of the air surrounding them.

All in all there are over one thousand, five hundred species of crickets, ranging in length from an eighth of an inch to over two inches. The antennae of the Gryllidae are even more noticeable than those of the grasshoppers, especially those grasshoppers of the family Acrididae. In most other respects they are quite similar to the Acrididae, having well-developed hind legs for jumping, tarsi containing three joints, and generally two slender abdominal cerci, although these may not be present in all species. The wings in many species of crickets are not fully developed, and crickets rarely fly. The forewings bear

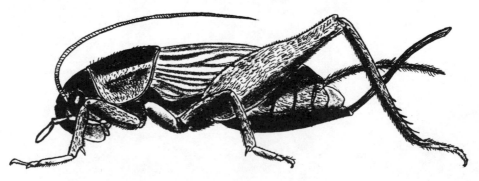

Field Cricket

Letort Cricket

Deer Hair Cricket

a certain resemblance to the wing cases of the Acrididae, being leathery and thick, with striations similar to normal wing venation. Only the rear wings are the flying organs, and these are never displayed unless the cricket is actually in flight.

The crickets, however, despite their family classifications, are far more than simply black grasshoppers. While grasshoppers are frequently caught and sold for bait, millions of crickets are actually reared each year by bait sellers, just as earthworms are reared, and the market for them is a little-known but very important industry. The ability to rear them, and their effect upon various game fish in the live state, make the cricket imitations that much more important in the terrestrial fisherman's repertoire: artificials cost less to tie than live crickets cost to purchase; and the imitations last far longer than the soft-bodied naturals.

In point of fact, the cricket is, if anything, more effective than the grasshopper, although the grasshopper imitations are used far more frequently. The reason for this greater effectiveness is that the crickets are indeed softer-bodied than their cousins the tobacco spitters, and therefore more succulent, and, as well, they fall into the water less frequently and so are struck with greater abandon than their more prevalent family members.

As a point of interest, the cricket is also a very popular laboratory insect in many areas of the world, and more crickets are used in experiments than guinea pigs, hamsters, and mice put together. The Oriental peoples have always used the crickets for other purposes than fish bait as well; in China the males are caged and kept solely for their songs, while throughout the Asian countries, crickets are captured and raised for the purpose of participating in cricket fights— a sport as big in the Orient as pit bullfights and cockfights used to be in the United States before they were outlawed.

There are many many species of crickets, but the species most important for the fisherman is the field cricket, subfamily Gryllinae, genus *Gryllus*. These crickets are generally about an inch in length, and are the most common and widely distributed of the crickets that fish feed upon. They also are the most easily found of all the insects for direct duplication, since they occur in fields, meadows, forests, lawns, and even along the roadside. In the summer, crickets can usually be found by turning over boards or fallen logs in grassy places; the light seems to stun them for a moment when they are first exposed, and they can be easily captured in the hand. Crickets can do a great deal of damage to rugs and clothing, but they are totally harmless to man insofar as stinging, biting, or scratching is concerned.

Technically there are many different species of *Gryllus*, but since scientists themselves used to believe that all field crickets were of the same species, it is pretty obvious that the fine line between the species need not concern the terrestrial fisherman. All the various species are almost identical in appearance to all intents and purposes, and the major classification differences involve life history, song, and habitat rather than physical characteristics.

Because of the distinct similarity between the crickets and their cousins the grasshoppers, it is possible to use any of the grasshopper patterns, using all black materials as substitutes for the various hues of the grasshopper, as representing the crickets. However, some are more effective than others, and for that reason the following two specific patterns are offered:

THE LETORT CRICKET

The Letort Cricket is tied in precisely the same manner as the Letort Hopper, and I cannot advise too strongly the addition of at least a half dozen of each pattern to the fly boxes. For some reason this rather impressionistic pattern seems to draw the fish from low water or high, in sun or shade, in rough water or calm. The pattern is as follows:

> Hook: #'s 8, 10, regular or 2X long (Mustad #94842 or #9671).
> Thread: Black.
> Abdomen: Black dyed muskrat or black Poly-X dubbing material.
> Thorax: Same as abdomen, with definite separation. (The body of the cricket should be tied much fuller than that of the hopper, since crickets generally have much broader bodies for their length than do their orthopteran relatives.)
> Underwing: Black crow wing quill section, cut in one piece, coated with rubber cement, and wrapped around the body, allowing only the base of the body to show.
> Wing: Black deer hair tied over crow wing quill section and slightly flared.
> Head: The butts of the deer hair wing flared fully and kept on top of the hook. Trim to shape.

As you can see from the list of materials, the Letort Cricket is basically the same as the Letort Hopper, only tied completely in black. The thread is started 1/3 of the way back from the eye of the hook and carried to a point opposite the barb. Then the black fur dubbing (or Poly-X material) is spun onto the thread and wound smoothly back and forth until a smooth, full, cigar-shaped body is formed. This is one fly in which the dressing of the body cannot possibly be too full. The larger the body, the more succulent the artificial appears. When you consider that these crickets, while only slightly more than an inch in length in real life, are often 3/8" to 1/2" in breadth, you can see the point in not scrimping on the body material. The body is ended at a point 1/3 of the length of the hook back from the eye, where the thread was originally started.

The underwing is added at this point. A section of crow wing quill, 1/2" to 5/8" in width, is cut from a flight feather, evened up as much as possible, and coated with rubber cement. As in the case of the grasshopper imitations, the rubber cement provides durability while still allowing complete flexibility. After the rubber cement has dried, the section of quill is centered on top of, and wrapped around, the body material, so that only the bottom of the body can be seen. This serves two purposes: it provides greater protection for the fly; and it gives a more realistic appearance to the cricket imitation in the water, since crickets, even in the water, open their wings far less frequently than do grasshoppers.

The overwing is then tied on in the same manner as prescribed for the Letort Hopper. A bunch of black deer hair is cut from the skin, and laid on top of the hook. The thread is then wrapped lightly around the hair and the shank of the hook, twice, to prevent spinning. Still holding the hair firmly on top of the body with the thumb and forefinger, tighten the thread, causing the hair to flare but not to revolve around the shank of the hook. Still holding the hair in place, crisscross the thread back and forth through the short stubs of the hair that flare toward the eye of the hook, making certain that all the hairs flare upward. Finish off the head with a whip finish (five turns of thread around the half-hitch tool) and coat liberally with head cement, allowing the cement to soak into the base of the hair forming the head.

Now trim the head at a 45° angle from the eye of the hook upward toward the wing, and the Letort Cricket is complete. If desired, black head cement can be used, but in my experience I have found that, if the proper color of thread is used in all patterns, clear cement does the job perfectly, and the practice of keeping the right colors of thread on hand is far less expensive in the long run than trying to stock a full line of different colors of head cement, which has a tendency to get thick, or even hard, if not watched carefully.

DEER HAIR CRICKET

The Deer Hair Cricket is, in effect, similar to the Deer Hair Hopper, with a very few exceptions. The fact is that crickets, when they land on the water, have a tendency to hold their legs (the kicking legs) together, supporting themselves with the four walking legs, instead of splaying out all six legs as do the grasshoppers. This action is true nine times out of ten (or, if you wish to be technical, ninety-two times out of one hundred according to my own test). Therefore, in order to be effective the deer hair cricket (or any cricket imitation for that matter) does not need to display the kicking legs as do most of the grasshopper imitations.

The deer hair cricket is simpler than the deer hair hopper therefore, in some respects, although there are certain differences. Since the antennae of the natural crickets are more evident than the antennae of the Acrididae, it is necessary in the case of the deer hair cricket to at least suggest the antennae. However, rather than tying in peccary or other hair or feathers for the walking legs and the antennae, it is possible to utilize the deer hair itself to suggest these appendages thus creating the entire fly out of deer hair and thread. The components, therefore, are as follows:

Hook:#'s 6, 8, 2X or 3X long (Mustad #9671).
Thread: Black.
Abdomen: Black deer hair.
Thorax: Same as abdomen.
Underwing: None.
Wing: None.
Legs: Fibers of deer hair cemented together.

Head: Black deer hair.
Antennae: Fibers of deer hair cemented together.

The deer hair is spun on the hook as in the case of the Deer Hair Hopper, starting the thread at the bend of the hook and spinning on one bunch after another on the bare hook shank, making certain that each bunch is pushed, as firmly as possible, against the bunch immediately behind it to give a very tight body.

The major difference comes in the trimming. Two-thirds of the way forward from the bend of the hook, leave at least ten hairs sticking out laterally from the body, at full length. When trimming the head, allow a fringe of hair to extend at a 45° angle upward from the trimmed head of the fly, again the full length of the hair used to tie the fly.

Divide the fringes at the side of the fly into two equal parts per side (approximately four or five hairs per part) and, applying head cement or nail polish to the fingers, stroke each bunch together so that there are two distinctly separate points of hair coming from each side of the fly to represent the walking legs.

Using the cement in the same manner, form the antennae at the head, trimming out any excess hairs in between the two formed antennae. Whip finish the head of the fly, and saturate thoroughly with very thin head cement to reinforce the thread windings. The deer hair cricket is complete.

The cricket imitations are especially effective in streams that pass through woodlands. If you are not on a fly-fishing-only stream, one sure way to catch fish is to throw a few live crickets into the water and then drift an imitation along after them. Both trout and bass will strike these imitations with abandon if presented in such a manner, and the cricket patterns make excellent searching flies as well, often drawing bass or lunker trout out of overhangs when all conventional flies fail.

6

WOOLLY WORMS

The Woolly Worm fly has been around for a long time, and is recognized as one of the best flies that has ever been created, especially when fishing streams, lakes, creeks, or ponds where the trees or bushes overhang the water. The Woolly Worm is not, technically, an insect in its own right. Rather, it is the larval form of the Lepidoptera, or butterflies—in plain language, the Woolly Worm is a caterpillar.

Lepidoptera is the technical term for the family of insects consisting of butterflies and moths. For many years fly fishermen have used massive bass bugs resembling moths, but in point of fact the larval stages of these insects are more readily taken than are the adults. The caterpillars are the major stage in transformation, which is a complete metamorphosis, from egg to caterpillar through pupae to adult butterfly or moth. The caterpillar stage is the stage most likely to land in the water, which explains the preference of the fish for caterpillars over any other stage in development of the Lepidoptera.

If the student of fly duplication wishes to be technical, then the name *caterpillar* is inaccurate, although common. Scientifically, this stage in the metamorphosis of the butterfly or moth is called a Lepidopterous larva, and the flytier who wishes to pursue an interesting

Tent Caterpillar (Woolly Worm)

specialty can find as many different patterns to duplicate from life in the realm of the caterpillar as there are patterns in this entire book. For the purposes of practicality, however, there are four primary patterns that are effective over a wide range of habitats and fishing conditions, and they provide a good jumping-off point for the student of the Woolly Worms.

Caterpillars are generally cylindrical in shape, and possess six thoracic legs, which will become the legs of the adult butterfly or moth after pupation, as well as ten or fewer soft, fleshly protuberances on the abdomen called abdominal prolegs. They do not possess the compound eyes of the adults, but generally have several small ocelli on each side of the head.

The varied appearance of certain caterpillars is what lends them to experimental duplication. Many are covered with bristly hair or spines, while others are smooth or leathery. In addition, many species are brightly ornamented with intense color, and some even resemble other creatures in order to frighten away predators. In general, caterpillars are completely safe to handle, although there are a few of the bristly variety that carry a mild toxin in the bristles, again to discourage predators, that will irritate the skin if the larvae are handled roughly.

Many caterpillars possess silk glands, with which they spin their cocoons, but very few are of commercial importance in that respect. Rather, the greatest commercial importance of the Lepidopterous larvae is negative, in that many species are highly destructive of cultivated plants, notably vegetables and fruit trees; some even attack stored and processed grains. Live bait fishermen never have any trouble in obtaining the permission of farmers and gardeners to remove several dozen of the creatures from growing crops.

But there are certain disadvantages to utilizing the live larvae that can be overcome through the use of artificial duplicates. First, artificials

Woolly Worms

do not have to be kept alive: they don't have to be kept cool, and no food is necessary. Second, artificials are no where near as messy to handle as their living counterparts: the most effective way (according to some fishermen) of using the live caterpillars, notably the Catalpa Worms, is to turn them inside out; and even without going to this extreme, the act of running a hook through the very juicy bodies of these creatures is a messy job in itself. Third, the use of artificials permits the application of these very effective patterns to fly-fishing only streams, where all live bait is forbidden.

The first two patterns presented here are what I call suggestive patterns, in that they represent a wide variety of caterpillars rather than duplicating any particular species. The remaining two are duplicating patterns, representing the Woolly Bear caterpillar and the very popular Catalpa Worm. Unless you can actually see and identify the variety of caterpillar present on bushes overhanging the water, the first two patterns make excellent searching flies; however, if caterpillars are in evidence and duplicable, by all means match them as closely as possible—fish can be as particular about these succulent morsels of the insect world as they can about the minute mayfly patterns of the "match the hatch" fraternity.

PATTERN I

Pattern I is the basic Woolly Worm as it was developed many years ago. It is exceptionally simple to tie, and imitates in general all of the bristly varieties of caterpillars. Three colors cover the general range, and hook sizes can range from very small to quite large.

Pattern I

Hook: #'s 2–10, 3X long (Mustad #9672).
Thread: Red.
Body: Yellow, brown, or black chenille.
Ribbing: Grizzly hackle.
Tail: Red wool yarn.

Affix the hook in the vise and start the thread just behind the eye. Wind it back to a point opposite the barb and half-hitch. Bind in a ¼″ length of medium red wool yarn for the tail, and half-hitch securely. This "tail" is imitative of nothing whatsoever, since cater-pillars don't have tails as such, but the red color does seem to attract fish, either from the brightness of the yarn itself or because the fish thinks that the red is actually part of the entrails of the caterpillar trailing out behind it.

Now tie in a length of medium-sized chenille in either yellow, brown, or black. It is a good plan to make up a few in each color, since the yellow chenille covers naturals in all shades of cream through yellow, the brown covers most of the browns and greens, and the black takes care of dark gray through pure black. At the same time that you tie in the chenille, tie in a 4" grizzly (Plymouth Rock) hackle, and wind the thread forward to just behind the eye.

Now wrap the chenille around the hook to ⅛" behind the eye, half-hitch it, and trim off the excess. Using hackle pliers, spiral the grizzly hackle forward in even turns approximately 3/16" to ¼" apart, depending upon the size of the hook. Tie it off at the head, trim away any surplus, build up a moderate head with the tying thread, and whip finish. Coat the head heavily with fly-tying cement to give a smooth, glossy finish and the fly is complete.

PATTERN II

With the use of a stiff and glossy grizzly hackle, Pattern I makes an excellent dry fly style of Woolly Worm, one especially effective in the smaller sizes. It is designed to be fished when the caterpillars are being held in the surface tension. But the problem is that, especially in late summer when the water is low and clear, fish will not always rise to take a dry fly, no matter how juicy it looks. The solution is to put the Woolly Worms at the same level as the fish, and that involves altering the materials.

Pattern II

Hook: #'s 8–12, 3X long (Mustad #38941).
Thread: Red.
Underbody: .010 lead wire.
Body: Yellow, brown, or black chenille.
Ribbing: Soft brown hen hackle.
Tail: Red wool yarn.

Pattern II is tied in precisely the same manner as Pattern I, the only exception being that, when the materials are tied in at the bend of the hook the lead wire is tied in at the same time, wound to a position 3/16" behind the eye, and trimmed to length. The thread is then wound over it, and the windings saturated with clear nail polish and allowed to dry before the chenille and brown hen hackle are brought forward.

The nail polish slows up the tying process briefly, but it is necessary to prevent discoloration of the materials. The problem with lead wire is that, after repeated immersions and drying out, the surface of the lead will oxidize, and the oxidation will, in time, stain the chenille. Sealing the lead against the elements with the nail polish will protect the body of the fly until it is torn apart by ravenous fish. The soft, brown hackle will help get the fly down in the water, and the action of water current and rod action will cause the soft fibers to undulate enticingly. If you have any dry Woolly Worms, which you certainly should if you want fish, you should match both color and size with the "wet" variety as well, so that you can go from top to bottom of the water you're fishing with no problems.

WOOLLY BEAR

The Woolly Bear caterpillar is the larva of several varieties of moths falling under the family Actiidae, or Tiger Moths. The most common members of this family are the Banded Woolly Bear Moth (*Isia isabella*), the Salt-Marsh Caterpillar (*Estigmene acraea*), and the Virgin Tiger Moth (*Apantesis virgo*). The larvae of all species

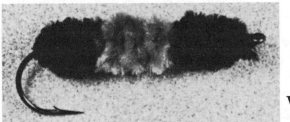

Woolly Bear

of the Arctiidae are similar in appearance, being quite hairy or bushy. These are also the caterpillars that are supposed to predict the degree and duration of winter by the width of their bands of color. There are two methods of tying the Woolly Bear, one dry pattern and one wet.

Dry: Hook: #'s 2–6, 3X long (Mustad #9672).
        Thread: Black.
        Rear Band: Black deer hair.
        Center Band: Brown or green deer hair.
        Front Band: Black deer hair.

The deer hair is spun on the shank in the same manner in which the Deer Hair Hopper and the Deer Hair Cricket are made, with the thread started at the bend of the hook and the hair spun around the bare shank to facilitate both the spinning and the flaring. Shove each bunch of hair back firmly against the previous bunch, half-hitch the thread, and apply a drop of thinned head cement so that it penetrates the base of the hair. This is one fly that has to take a tremendous beating. The point to bear in mind is that the center band of brown or green should be twice the length of either the rear or the forward band—in other words, the center band makes up $\frac{1}{2}$ the length of the hook, while each of the black bands account for $\frac{1}{4}$ the length.

After the hair is flared and cemented, even up the ends with a pair of scissors, but do not trim too closely. The fly must be bushy, and it should appear prickly.

Wet: Hook: #'s 4–8, 3X long (Mustad #9672).
            Thread: Black.
            Rear Band: Black chenille.
            Center Band: Brown or green chenille.
            Front Band: Black chenille.

The chenille Woolly Bear is perhaps the easiest fly in the entire book to tie. Use the heaviest chenille you can obtain and simply make three bands: 1 black, $\frac{1}{4}$ the length of the hook from the bend forward; 1 brown, $\frac{1}{2}$ the length of the hook from the end of the rear black band; and 1 black, $\frac{1}{4}$ the length of the hook from the front of the brown band to the eye. Tie it off, trim off any excess, whip finish a very small head, and apply a dab of head cement. The chenille will soak up water and carry the fly down, but since the fly is unweighted it won't dig into the bottom. It's as effective as it is simple.

CATALPA WORM

The Catalpa Worm is the favorite of fishermen, and the bane of catalpa tree owners. This caterpillar, when it appears in numbers, can strip the foliage of a catalpa tree within a matter of weeks. Its

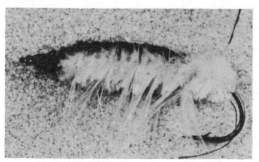

Catalpa Worm

sole redeeming feature is that fish seem to go insane when one of these caterpillars hits the water. I have yet to develop a pattern that looks like a Catalpa Worm turned inside out, but the following pattern looks sufficiently like the living insect to be taken with abandon by both bass and panfish.

Hook: #'s 4–10, 2X long (Mustad #9671).
Thread: Black.
Spine: Yellow stripped quill tip, marked with black felt-tip pen.
Body: Heavy yellow chenille with black wool stripe down back.
Legs: Yellow saddle hackle, clipped.

Affix the hook in the vise and start the thread at the eye, winding it evenly back to a point just opposite the barb of the hook. Take the stripped quill tip, and tie it in so that it extends upward and toward the rear of the hook. Half-hitch the quill section securely. Now tie in the chenille, a 4″ yellow saddle hackle, and a 2″ length of heavy black wool. Wind the chenille forward, first making one turn *behind* the quill section, and tie it off with three half-hitches.

Wind the hackle forward, tie it off with two half-hitches, and trim away any excess. Take the fine-pointed scissors and trim the hackle flat against the top of the chenille, and very close at the sides, leaving only a slightly bristly appearance, rather like an extension of some of the fibers of the chenille itself. Mark an imaginary straight line across the bottom of the hackles parallel to the hook shank, and trim away any fibers that extend below that line.

Now bring the black wool forward across the top of the fly and tie it in at the head. Trim away any excess, and whip finish and cement the head. The fly should now be taken from the vise, and a black felt-tipped pen used to mark the "spine" at the tail. The marker will not color the quill where the yellow dye remains—only the sides where the fibers were stripped off. The result is a mottled black and yellow spine that is quite effective. The Catalpa Worm can be fished either dry (with the liberal application of fly floatant) or wet, the chenille and wool soaking up water readily to get the fly down. Catalpa Worms themselves almost always sink when they land in the water unless they are small enough to be held by the surface tension, so I recommend the "wet" approach—let the fly behave as it wishes. In the smaller sizes the surface tension may hold it, but if it starts to sink, don't worry, just hold on. There may well be a fish below it just waiting for the Catalpa to give up and drown.

7
LANDFLIES

Smack! Both the bite and the slap threw my timing off, and my tapered line dumped into the water ten feet in front of me, the leader in a snarl and the fly sitting in the middle of the leader, tangled like a hapless creature caught in a spider web. I had already used up a great portion of my "nasty" vocabulary, so I flicked the mashed deerfly out into the water—and a ten-inch bluegill kicked water into my face as it grabbed the bloody insect. I thought briefly of the six-inchers I had been playing with on caddis imitations, and started pondering.

The next day I was back at the same slough hole with some crude horsehair imitations of the voracious deerfly. The bluegills didn't even take the time to decide whether or not the flies were exact imitations— they gobbled them as though they were having their last meal, which, indeed, a frying pan full of the largest ones were.

The episode with the bluegills got me thinking. There had been many times when the trout had refused my offerings of mayflies or caddis, while landflies had been doing their best to turn me anemic. With research and some more sophisticated tying, I came up with what I thought was a good selection of typical flies that plague fly-fishermen, but that they normally disregard.

The insects that I term *flies* in this book are the true flies of the order Diptera, as distinguished from the various other so-called aquatic flies (may, dobson, etc.) , which in fact belong to other orders and are not true flies at all. The land flies are distinguished by a single pair of membranous wings (hence the order name, Diptera, meaning two wings) . The antennae are frequently quite short, often scarcely noticeable, and formed in three segments. These virtually unnoticeable antennae are a boon to the flytier who is striving for close imitation,

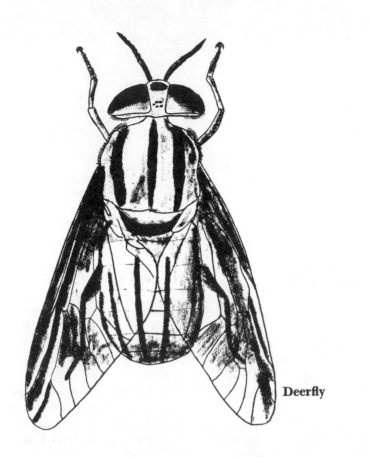

Deerfly

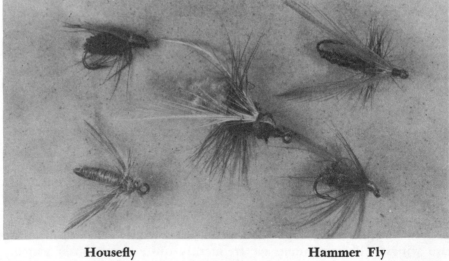

Housefly		Hammer Fly
	Horsefly	
Deerfly		Greenbottle Fly

66

since they can be readily omitted from the pattern at no cost whatsoever to its effectiveness.

Diptera have very large compound eyes, which sometimes meet at the top of the head. In any of the following patterns small beads can be attached to either end of a short wire and bound onto the shank of the hook just behind the hook eye, with the body material criss-crossed between them to fill in the head, should the tier be interested in precise duplication. These bead eyes are unnecessary to the effectiveness of the pattern, but their use makes an interesting addition for a wall display of the tier's talent. They should be slightly darker in color than the body material.

The larvae of these flies are called maggots, and although the most familiar maggots are those of the common housefly, all of the Diptera larvae are similar. Sometimes maggots are highly effective baits, and many pan-fishermen use the actual larvae. They can be duplicated effectively by the flytier simply by using a #10 to #14 hook, standard length, wrapped with a tapered body of white, cream, pale green, or tan latex material. A selection of these should be in every fly box, but since they are so rudimentary there need be no instruction in the tying.

For the entomologist's information, according to zoological sources there are approximately 86,000 species of Diptera throughout the world, and about 16,130 species on the North American continent alone. Many of these are bloodsuckers, as fishermen well know; a flytier could become very frustrated trying to duplicate all of the various landflies that might fall into the water.

Happily, fly-fishermen do not require 16,130 different patterns of landflies to be effective. Five patterns, with one variation, cover the field quite nicely, since they cover both the size and the color range of most of the flies commonly found around good waters. Because of the two-winged nature of the Diptera, the patterns are easy to tie, and at times when there is no insect life present upon the water or on the reeds near the water, one of the landflies can turn a fruitless trip into a success.

HAMMAR FLY

The hammar fly is a member of the family Rhagionidae, and is, along with the deerfly, one of the two most important terrestrial flies to the fly-fishermen, since it is what I term a transitional fly in that the larvae of some of the species of hammar fly are aquatic, often being found in rotting vegetation along the shoreline. The Eastern angler is more fortunate in regard to this family of flies than the Western angler, not because of any greater abundance of the creatures, but rather because the Eastern species do not bite, whereas some of the Western species are bloodsuckers. These are very common flies throughout the United States, occurring especially in wooded locales and places where the vegetation is quite thick. The Hammar Fly pattern (also called the Snipe Fly in some areas) is a very good pattern to have on hand for woodland streams and ponds, as well as for the shallow areas adjacent to marshes.

The hammar fly species vary from 5/16" to ⅝", and are mostly black and gray, although some have a touch of yellow on the thorax. This hint of yellow is again unnecessary for the tier and is added only as a note of interest to the amateur entomologist and to the display tier who desires a completely lifelike representation of each separate species. For the practical fisherman-tier, a black or dark gray body is just as effective.

The following pattern has proved effective on both trout and panfish.

> Hook: #'s 10, 12, 14, regular or light wire.
> Thread: Black.
> Body: Black raffia or latex, tied with definite segmentation. If raffia is used, it should be lacquered to provide a slight gloss, as well as strengthen the tie. Any shade of gray may also be used, with the exception of the very pale tones.
> Wings: Pale gray hackle tips. Iron blue dun is acceptable, though not quite as effective as the paler shades of gray.
> Legs: Black hackle wound palmer on front third of body, trimmed top and bottom.
> Head: Black tying thread, heavily lacquered to give hard, round appearance.

The Hammar Fly is not a difficult pattern, and the practice will make the other landflies in this section that much easier. The most important point to bear in mind is that the body should show definite segmentations, and should *not* be tied heavily. The hammar flies have slender bodies, tapering narrowly toward the posterior.

The hackle tip wings should be relatively pale in color, although they should be obviously gray in tone. They should be tied on a plane with the hook shank, at anywhere between a 30° to 45° angle to the line of the body, and positioned so that when the fly is on the water they will be flat against the surface tension. Since the hackle in the case of this pattern is trimmed to approximately ¼ the body length, the wings will provide the flotation, so the greater surface area in contact with the water, the longer the fly will float.

Either raffia or latex may be used for this pattern. My first experiments were with lacquered raffia, and for panfish it is still the preferred medium. However, in the case of trout, I have discovered that they will hold onto the latex body longer than they will the harder construction. Panfish attack with such gusto that the body material doesn't really seem to matter, although the latex body is perhaps a bit more durable, if not as shiny. Certainly, for the all-round fly-fishermen, I would recommend flies in both body styles. For the angler with limited resources, or the angler specifically after trout, I suggest latex bodies. They don't elicit quite as many strikes, but they hook more of the strikers.

Regardless of the material used for the body, lacquer the head heavily. All of the Diptera have large heads in relation to the size of their bodies, so that in addition to providing that much extra strength to the tie, the heavily lacquered head offers greater realism. Even with the gray bodies, the head should definitely be black.

DEERFLY

Deerflies are of the family *Tabanidae*, and are the scourge of early-morning and late-evening fishermen, especially those who seek their angling treasure around forested shores. The females of this species are the culprits, for they are bloodsucking insects that attack with a vengeance (and pain) not even known to the female mosquito (also the gender of the species that bites). The males dine on flowers, and are unimportant to the fly-fisherman, not only from the sense of personal discomfort, but also in the sense that they do not as commonly fall into the water as do the heavier, verge-oriented females.

These are medium-sized flies, ranging from 3/8" to 5/8" in length, and have relatively stout bodies. They are especially good terrestrial flies to use around swamps, marshes, and ponds, since the larvae are aquatic and the adults, particularly the females, generally stay very close to the water, where all manner of animals are prey to their bloodsucking tendencies. Deerflies range from brown to black in color, usually with a slight iridescence around the head, and the wings are sometimes spotted with black. The following pattern is of the most common species, and works well wherever deerflies are found.

Hook: #'s 8 to 12, regular.
Thread: Tan or brown.
Body: Brown horsehair, ribbed with darker brown thread to give the appearance of segmentation.
Wings: Ginger hackle tips, tied spent. In darker shades, when emulating deerflies with spotted wings, grizzly hackle points should be substituted.
Legs: Ginger hackle, heavy at thorax and trimmed top and bottom to extend outward from sides.
Head: Brown tying thread, slightly darker than body, heavily lacquered.

As you will have noticed by now, the landflies have the advantage of not requiring tails. Although the lack of fibers at the rear of the fly cuts down on the flotation of the fly, if it is desirous to fish this pattern—or, for that matter, any of the landfly patterns—on the surface, tie in an underbody of kapok to provide the necessary support. Landflies are generally more effective when fished wet, but if deerflies are in abundance and noticeable above the water, a few tied with the buoyant underbody might be handy to have on hand. They are, however, unnecessary to the effective use of the pattern.

Note that the body of this fly is made of horsehair, which is in reality the long hairs from the tail of the horse. Such hair is available in many brown tones, and any of the medium to dark shades will work. A tier would go insane trying to build up the fly body with single strands of hair, so the process involves tying in between six and ten hairs (depending upon the size of the hook) and winding them back and forth until the desired cigar-shaped body is obtained. Take care to wind the hairs flat rather than twisting them while winding. The segmentation on the abdomen of the deerfly is only barely noticeable, and the twisted hairs will provide too much of a separation between segments. Suggest the segments with a spiral of slightly darker tying silk after the body has been wound. Since the deerfly has a rather shiny appearance, coating the entire body with a gloss or semigloss lacquer gives a more realistic effect, as well as greater durability. Fish don't sip these flies lightly; they hit them hard, and if the fly is not securely tied it will begin to unravel after half a dozen or so strikes.

The deerfly pattern is in all likelihood the most effective of the landfly patterns for use on beaver pond brook trout, often producing strikes right in the middle of a mayfly hatch, and thus eliminating the need for the difficult and time-consuming "matching the hatch" that has plagued trout fishermen since the development of imitative flies. Remember that almost any insect found in the proximity of a body of water will be fed upon by fish in that water, and the juicier the insect, the more anxious a fish will be to strike.

HORSEFLY

The horsefly, like the deerfly, is a member of the family Tabanidae, is usually gray to black, and although the wings do not contain the dark spots common to some of the deerflies, in certain species the entire wings themselves are dark. Some species have iridescent green eyed, which give them the common name of greenheads in some locales.

All characteristics of the deerfly also apply to the horsefly, only to a greater extent since the horsefly is considerably larger—up to an inch in length. The horsefly has a fat, oval body, and certain adjustments must be made in the tying process to accommodate the natural shape of the insect.

Hook: #'s 2–8, regular or 2x long.
Thread: Black.

Body: Two lengths of 30-lb. test monofilament tied to the sides of the hook shank and wrapped with tying thread, overlaid with heavy dark gray chenille for the abdomen and dark gray to black muskrat fur for the thorax.

Wings: Dark blue dun hackle points, tied splayed.

Legs: Black hackle, tied palmer around thorax and trimmed top and bottom to give bristly appearance.

Head: Black or fluorescent green tying thread, heavily lacquered.

Bind the monofilament to each side of the hook shank, making certain that it remains at the sides. If you have trouble with the mono rolling to the top or bottom, apply a little Duco cement to the hook shank and wait until it is partially set before applying the mono. The mono should extend from a point directly behind the eye to the bend of the hook, since the entire body of the horsefly is oval in nature.

The chenille abdomen should extend from the bend of the hook two thirds of the length of the shank. Make it full. Half of the remaining length is the thorax, tied with dubbed muskrat fur for translucence, and palmered with black hackle. The hackle should be trimmed so that, while it extends full length to the sides, the top and bottom of the thorax will be covered with 1/32" to 1/16" bristles.

The head is then wrapped with thread in proportion to the rest of the body and heavily lacquered so that it looks like a piece of plastic. Floss can be used to build up the head to save both time and thread, but it should definitely be covered with several layers of thread before being lacquered, for durability.

For a floating version of the Horsefly, which has proved deadly on bass, especially in farm ponds around which the actual flies are plentiful, substitute gray deer hair for the chenille and monofilament. It is applied in the same manner as for the Deer Hair Hopper or Cricket, and can be trimmed to an oval shape. Roll-cast under overhanging trees, the Horsefly takes not only bass, but monstrous bluegills, as well.

HOUSEFLY

The Housefly is one of the simplest of the landfly patterns to tie as well as being the one landfly that everyone, whether they fish or not, has had some experience with. The housefly, *Musca domestica*, is of the family Muscidae of the division Schizophora of the Suborder Cyclorrhapha. It is a very common fly, and one of the most important of all flying pests since, although it does not bite, it breeds in filth and carries typhoid fever, dysentery, cholera, and many other diseases. Black in color and ranging from 1/4" to 3/8" in length, it is one of the most important artificials for panfish such as bluegills and crappies.

Hook: #'s 8–14.
Thread: Black.
Body: Fine black chenille.

Legs: Black hackle, sparse.
Wings: Veined wing material.
Head Black tying thread, lacquered heavily.

The body is wrapped with fine, black chenille until it is one third as thick as it is long. Three turns of black hackle are wound around the thorax (forward third of the body), and clipped top and bottom as in all of the other landfly patterns.

The veined wing material is a great boon to flytiers who are not bound by the "feather-fur" tradition, and who are interested in creating the most effective imitations possible. I would like to point out that veined wing material, available from many suppliers in sheets, and from Herter's, Inc., in preformed wing patterns, may be substituted for hackle tip wings on any of the patterns in this book. It is both highly effective and durable, and I recommend it especially for patterns with transparent wings.

Veined wing material is a thin, plastic sheet, very pliable, with a black, imprinted pattern very similar to the venation of insect wings, and, in sheet form, may be cut to any size or shape. For the housefly pattern, the shape is as follows:

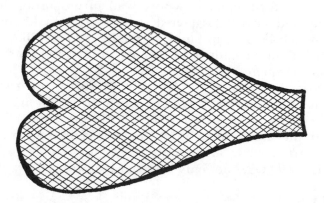

The size can be readily adjusted to the individual hook size. The pattern is then bent over the top of the hook shank to give the appearance of folded wings, bound in with the tying thread, and the tag end is trimmed. The head is then wrapped with black tying thread to the same diameter as the body, and heavily lacquered.

GREENBOTTLE FLY

The greenbottle fly, member of the family Calliphoridae, is a local name, though quite common, for one of the many species of blowflies. It is a very large family of flies, and commonly distributed. Most species are the same size as the housefly or slightly larger, and their bodies are of a metallic sheen. The eggs of the blowfly are laid in dead animals, fecal matter, and garbage, where they hatch into the larval form known as the maggot, mentioned earlier in this chapter. Most of these maggots feed only on dead flesh, and in doing so can help prevent infection in a wound by eating away the decaying flesh but leaving the healthy tissue. Some, however, such as the screw worm, also eat living tissue, and are a serious cause of death among livestock if not eradicated.

Since these creatures are serious pests around livestock, the fly pattern is effective in both farm ponds and in streams that wander through cow pastures, where the eggs are generally laid in the piles of cow dung. Both panfish and trout fall ready prey to blowfly imitations, as well as to imitations of the larval form, or maggot. When I was a boy, my friends and I used to root out the live maggots, and catch stringers full of bluegills—big bluegills—by threading the larva on a #12 hook. With the rashness of youth somewhere in the past, I now prefer artificial maggots, and notice only a slight decrease in their effectiveness.

A close relative of the greenbottle fly is the bluebottle fly, which can be tied to the same pattern with very slight variation.

Hook: #'s 8–12.
Thread: Dark brown.
Body: Light green or yellow kapok dubbing under pale green
    thread under green peacock herl.
Legs: Dark blue dun hackle, trimmed top and bottom.
Wings: Light blue dun hackle tips.
Head: Medium green thread, heavily lacquered.

The variation for the Bluebottle Fly uses the metallic blue peacock herl found in the eye of the feather, over dark blue thread over pale blue kapok, with the head blue rather than green. Wings and legs are the same on both patterns, and veined wing material can be substituted for the blue dun hackle tips. The kapok provides flotation, since these flies seem to be blown onto the water in a living state more readily and often than their other landfly associates.

Landflies should definitely be in every terrestrial fisherman's boxes, in a variety of patterns and sizes. I was first turned on to the effectiveness of landflies by my father, who used to catch horseflies in his hand when they were about to light on him, squeeze them enough to immobilize them but not crush them, and then use the living flies as bait on small hooks. Then the lure of the mayfly and the caddis caught me, and I forgot the abandon with which panfish and trout had struck the larger and more succulent Diptera. It took me a long time to remember, but now I wouldn't pick up the long rod without a few of the landfly patterns in a box along with it.

An interesting trick to use in heavily wooded streams where typical casting procedure is impossible is to take one of the deerfly patterns, stand back from the water, shove the tip of the rod through the trees, and dangle the fly just above the water, making it "hover." The method may not have much finesse, but it gets to water otherwise unavailable. Just make certain that your tippet is strong (see section on tackle). You may be surprised at what comes out of the water to grab your "flying" insect.

8
BEES

I had been hearing the sounds and smacks of surface feeding bluegills for half an hour—periodic *glurps* as the fish rose in the shallows to take something off the surface—but I was cleaning up from a shore dinner, and didn't pay too much attention. Finally the work was done, and I decided to see where all the activity was—only to find out that I had created it myself with an old camper's trick. That trick put me onto a few new fly patterns that have taken bluegills and bass for me ever since.

Every camper, especially those who do their cooking out of doors, knows what it is like to be plagued by bees and wasps that come to the smells of fish and other cooking. Yellow jacket wasps are the worst, but there is a way to eliminate virtually all but a few stragglers from the campsite. Simply take a fish—bluegill, perch, shad, or the like— and suspend it from a tree over a bucket of water. The wasps engorge themselves on the fish, fall into the bucket, and drown. I generally simply tie the fish on a limb that extends over the lake or stream, and that is precisely what I had done that evening. When I located the source of the commotion and crept close to the shore, the crystal-clear water revealed several nice bluegills lying directly under their suspended cousin, racing each other to the prize every time a wasp dropped from the hanging fish into the water.

Bees and wasps are of the order Hymenoptera, and are characterized by rather large bodies, four membranous wings, generally long antennae, and the possession of a stinger in many instances and biting mouth parts in others, either defense containing some sort of venom. There are over 105,000 species of bees and wasps throughout the world, and approximately 16,300 species in the United States alone. In all

Bumblebee
Honeybee

honesty, these are not the most generally effective patterns; however, where wasp nests are found, or where beehive trees are located close to bodies of water, they do take fish. They are what I term *optional patterns,* to be included in small numbers and used to duplicate what may be on or around the water, rather than as a general searching pattern. The bumblebee pattern is frequently excellent as a bass bug.

HONEYBEE

The honeybee, *Apis mellifera,* is the most common bee, and also the insect of greatest commercial importance. They are the furry bees that are responsible for the production of honey as well as for the effective pollination of most crops. In fact, farming and the raising of orchard crops would be almost impossible without the honeybee; its life history is a fascinating study to anyone interested in entomology. In addition, it is the only insect commercially reared. Honeybees range up to ¾" in length.

> Hook: #'s 8–10, regular.
> Thread: Brown.
> Abdomen: Alternate bands of yellow and brown chenille, size fine or extra-fine.
> Thorax: Medium brown chenille
> Wings: Ginger hackle tips.

Legs: Brown hackle, trimmed top and bottom.
Head: Brown tying thread.

The abdomen should be egg shaped, with its smaller end at the bend of the hook, but with a definite dip between the abdomen and thorax. Ideally, the bands of yellow and brown should not spiral, but rather should be wrapped separately. The extra time spent in carrying out this maneuver makes a much more realistic-looking bee.

The thorax should be relatively heavy, with the longer fibers of the medium chenille giving a hairy appearance. The wings should be tied along the top of the thorax, extending slightly outward toward the tail, and the head, slightly separated from the thorax, should be of the same diameter as the thorax. As in the case of the flies, floss may be used to give a rapid buildup to the head, but it should be finished off with a good overlay of tying thread and cemented for durability.

There is only one species of honeybee in the United States, and the above pattern is effective across the country. In some locales the colors differ slightly—not enough to affect the effectiveness of the pattern, but should the fanatic imitator so desire, these insects can be found in any lawn, and the colors, ranging from yellow through tan and cream, may be altered to suit the locale.

BUMBLEBEE

The bumblebee is a large, heavy bee, reaching an inch in length. It is black and yellow, sometimes with orange markings in certain species, but with yellow predominating. Bumblebees do not have the commercial importance of the honeybee, for they do not make honey in sufficient quantity to be economically valuable, and bumblebees of the genus *Psithyrus* do not even collect pollen, and hence are of no value to farmers for pollination.

Bumblebees are robust-looking insects, and are very hairy in appearance. They are more aggressive than their smaller relatives, although bumblebee stings do not seem to have a greater toxicity than honeybees, as would seem to be suggested by their greater size. The following pattern is a wet fly.

Hook: #6, 2x long.
Thread: Black.
Tag: Heavy black chenille.
Abdomen: Heavy yellow chenille, wound full.
Thorax: Heavy black chenille, with one turn of heavy yellow
    chenille just behind the head.
Wings: Ginger hackle tips.
Legs: Black hackle wound on thorax heavily and trimmed top
    and bottom.
Head: Black tying thread.

77

The bumblebee is not striped as is the honeybee, but it does possess a black tail and a yellow band between the thorax and head. Since the legs of the bumblebee are very stout, the hackle should be wound heavily so that an ample amount extends outward on either side of the fly after the top and bottom are trimmed.

The wet pattern is effective, but because of the size of the fly and the necessity of a large, full body, the chenille soaks up water rapidly and makes casting difficult. The Bumblebee can also be tied as a dry fly-bass bug, which, although having more wind resistance because it is lighter in proportion to its size, nevertheless is easier to cast because it resists soaking. A selection of both patterns can usually take bass or large bluegills and crappie, since the former pattern can be used if no surface feeding is in evidence, and the following, dry pattern employed when the fish are dimpling the surface.

Hook: #6, 2x long.
Thread: Black.
Tag: Black deer hair, spun and clipped to shape.
Abdomen: Yellow deer hair, spun and clipped to shape.
Thorax: Black deer hair, with yellow deer hair collar between thorax and head, spun and clipped to shape, leaving several long hairs extending from sides of thorax.
Wings: Ginger hackle tips.
Legs: Long black deer hair from sides of thorax, divided into three equal parts on each side and each part stroked together with cement.
Head: Black tying thread.

The dry pattern takes longer to tie than the wet pattern, but is well worth the extra effort. The hair is spun in the same manner as applied to the various other deer hair creations in the book, notably the grasshoppers and crickets. It should be packed tight, and, when barbering the creation to its final shape, a layer of hair along each side of the thorax, about three hairs deep and extending the full length of the thorax, should be let at full length.

To create the legs, use a bodkin to separate the rear third of the fringe hair on one side from the forward two thirds. Holding the hair apart with the bodkin, stroke a dab of Duco cement through the rear third, twisting the hair together and pulling it toward the rear. Hold until tacky. Now divide the remaining fringe in half and do the same thing to the forward third of the fringe, pulling it toward the head. Hold until set, and then stroke and twist the middle third with some glue, leaving it extending straight out from the side. Do the same with the fringe on the other side, and the Deer Hair Bumblebee is complete.

WASPS

Wasps differ from bees in being more slender, more elongated, less hairy, and generally more aggressive. While bees seldom will attack unless actually physically disturbed, wasps will often attack, either singly or in numbers, anyone who approaches too closely their nesting area. There are few sportsmen who have not at one time or another stumbled upon a nest of yellow jackets, white-faced hornets, or paper wasps, and the experience is not one likely to be forgotten.

YELLOW JACKETS

Yellow jackets are the species of wasp most commonly encountered by anglers, since they are quite common in both woods and the verges of small to large bodies of water. The abdomen is banded with black and yellow, so that many people quite commonly mistake these wasps for bees. Their nests are built of a papery material forming the larval cells, generally with an outer covering, and they nest quite often in holes in the ground or at the bases of hollow trees. Yellow jackets are quite fond of coming around anglers' campsites, especially if fish are being cleaned; they will not hesitate to attack if the fish cleaner swats at them, and they can inflict a very painful sting.

Hook: #'s 6–10, 2X long.
Thread: Black.
Abdomen: Yellow raffia wound over kapok underbody, with black
    enamel markings as shown in illustration.
Thorax: Black silk flosswound full.
Wings: Ginger hackle tips.
Legs: Ginger, clipped top and bottom.
Head: Black tying thread.

Since the bands of color on a yellow jacket's abdomen are not full and large as in the case of the honeybee, black enamel can best be used to delineate them, as shown in the illustration below:

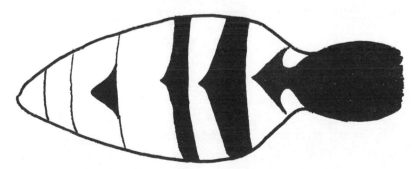

Raffia provides an excellent base for the enamel, since the paint will not bleed into the rest of the tie as it would with almost any other sort of body material. The thorax is pure black and glossy, and should be wound of silk floss to obtain the proper rounding of the tie. Acetate floss, sometimes called "hardshell" floss by a few suppliers, makes an excellent thorax. It can either be left plain, or dipped into the acetone solution to melt and harden it. If it is to be dipped, do the dipping before adding the abdominal markings, however, since the chemical action of the acetone will affect some paints and cause them to run.

The head is to be wound full and black. If acetate floss is used for the thorax, the head may also be made of this material, showing definite separation from the thoraxial area, and then dipped. This will provide a very strong and virtually indestructible fly head.

The wings should be tied so as to lie flat along the sides of the thorax and abdomen, and the hackle for the legs is wound between the thorax and abdomen in a narrow band—*not* palmered.

Any wasp can be duplicated by using the general construction methods outlined for the Yellow Jacket, and by simply changing the colors to suit the individual species. The other common wasp encountered most often in fishing areas is the white-faced hornet. Tying methods are precisely the same, but to give you an idea of how other wasp patterns are created, the pattern for the White-Faced Hornet is as follows:

Hook: #'s 6–10, 3X long.
Thread: Black.
Tag: White raffia, same thickness as abdomen.
Abdomen: Black raffia, wound over kapok underbody.
Thorax: Black raffia, with white enamel marking on front half.
Head: Black tying thread with front half painted white.
Wings: Blue dun hackle tips.
Legs: Black hackle.

9
WORMS

The two Worm patterns in this short chapter could conceivably fall under the heading of Woolly Worms in other books. However, I have separated them for the simple reason that Woolly Worms are very common patterns, and are designed to imitate the larger caterpillars, in particular the catalpa worms and woolly bear caterpillars. Although these two patterns represent caterpillars as well, they are so completely different from the commonly accepted concept of the Woolly Worm that I feel they deserve to be separated in nomenclature as well as technique.

The two Worm patterns are relative delineations of the larvae of the Geometer moths, often called inchworms or measuring worms. They are an extremely large group of insects, with over twelve hundred species common to North America alone, and are found in almost every locale. The larvae are small, slender caterpillars, almost exclusively a pale green in color, and they move in a looping fashion by holding the forelegs clamped to the stalk or leaf of a plant and walking up toward their own heads with their hind legs. They then lift the fore portion of their bodies and, due to the loop made by their rear action, push the forward part of their bodies forward until they are fully extended.

These larvae feed on all sorts of plants, and in some cases can do extensive damage to orchard and shade trees. They are especially effective patterns for panfish and trout, since in their process of inching their way along limbs and grasses that overhang the water they frequently are unseated by the wind and fall onto the water's surface. Since they are soft and juicy, they are readily taken by small to medium-sized fish, and occasionally by very large trout. These patterns,

81

one wet and the other floating, seem to be taken with great gusto rather than being merely "sipped" in, and in the case of panfish the fish will often hook themselves on the strike if the hook is kept needle sharp.

WORM—WET PATTERN

The wet pattern is most effective in flowing water, such as is found in most trout waters. It should be fished on a dead drift, as though drowned, cast up and across stream, and allowed to roll with the current, keeping a tight line.

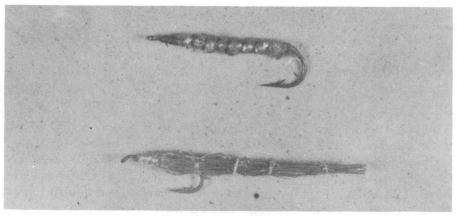

Worm-Wet Pattern
Worm-Dry Pattern

Hook: #'s 10–14, 3X long.
Thread: Pale green.
Body: Green raffia or latex, wound over built up tying thread body, and lapped to give the effect of light segmentation.
Legs: None.
Head: Pale green tying thread, lacquered.

Since raffia is relatively brittle, even when soaked, and does not make the smoothest of bodies when wrapped on a bare hook shank, the underbody should be built up as smoothly as possible to approximately 1/16″ in diameter, and the raffia, well soaked, wrapped smoothly over it. The body does not have to be tapered, but the raffia should overlap slightly to give the impression of segmentations. In addition to the segmental appearance, the slight overlap helps keep the fly going longer, since any slight movement of the material backward or forward due to the strikes of fish will still leave the rest of the body completely covered.

Latex should be wrapped in the same manner, and can be substituted for the raffia with no loss in effectiveness of the fly. However, due to the very elastic nature of the latex, the underbody of thread should first be covered with a thin coat of cement to eliminate the showing of the thread wraps under the overlay. Make certain that the thread is perfectly smooth before applying the latex, and then proceed as explained for the raffia. Latex is easier to work with, since it does not need to be soaked and wraps more smoothly. The raffia body is traditional. The choice is up to the individual tier.

Although this is a wet pattern, it should not be weighted. Inch-worms are extremely light caterpillars that will float in the surface tension before sinking slowly to the bottom, and in waters where a current is present they are carried rapidly along with the flow. The fly pattern should imitate this susceptibility, and a weighted fly will drag bottom and hang up more often than the slowly sinking un-weighted pattern.

WORM—DRY PATTERN

The dry pattern gains most of its effectiveness in still waters, such as ponds or lakes. There it will take trout, when present, and enough panfish from bluegills to perch to keep the fly-rodder busy for hours. It will also take largemouth bass on occasion, particularly when fished around fallen trees, although the bass that hit the dry inchworm are usually in the one-half- to two-pound category rather than the lunkers taken on some of the other patterns in this book.

Hook: #'s 10–14, regular or 2X long.
Thread: Pale green.
Body: Green dyed deer hair, tied with loops of thread to simulate segmentation.
Legs: None.
Head: Pale green tying thread, lacquered.

Bucktail may be substituted for the green deer hair, although it is not as buoyant and generally darker in shade when dyed. The hair should be between 2½ and 3″ in length, and should be laid along the hook so that the butt ends extend 1½ to 2″ past the eye. Bind it securely as you roll the hair around the shank, so that the shank is completely covered.

Wrap the thread to approximately ⅛″ behind the eye, and draw all of the hair back along the sides of the hook evenly, tying it off to form a bulbous head of deer hair. Cover this head with pale green silk tying thread for strength.

Keep moving the thread backward ⅛″ at a time, binding down the hair at each point to make segments, until the bend of the hook is reached. Tie off the thread, and cut it.

Now, from the bend of the hook to the end of the hair, pull the hairs together with loops of thread every ⅛″ to form an extended segmented body, until the ends of the hairs are reached. Trim away the ends of the thread loops, as well as any flyaway hairs, and lacquer each of the windings as well as the head.

This is an extremely durable fly that will float for a long time before needing treatment with fly dope. The extended body puts the point of the hook near the middle of the body, thus assuring more consistent hooking, in addition to the fact that the fly will bend in a fish's mouth, giving a greater feeling of reality, and hence less chance of the fly being spit out.

10
ANTS

The proponents of fur and feathers may thank their lucky stars that they will never be limited to a single pattern of fly. A great part of the enjoyment of fly-fishing and fly tying is the discovery of what insects the fish are eating at any given moment, and the subsequent successful duplication of those insects with artificials to the point where the fish are taken in. Nevertheless, were we to actually be limited to a single pattern, I would have to choose the ant in its various simple modifications. With the various ant patterns I have taken almost every species of fish likely to be encountered in fresh or brackish water, with the exception of the various species of pike, which are seldom taken on the fly rod, using anything save streamer-type minnow imitations.

Ants, like bees and wasps, are of the order Hymenoptera, possessing,

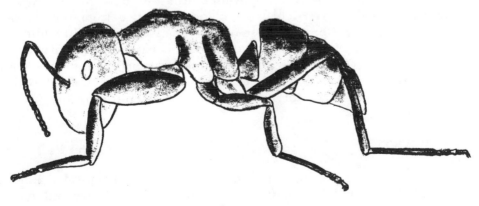

Ant

85

where present, two pairs of pale, veined wings. Only a few species of ants, such as the velvet ant and fire ant, sting, and most of the ants have their mouth parts developed into strong mandibles, or pinching jaws. Ants belong to the family Formicidae, and are most notable for the definite separation of the three parts of the body: head, thorax, and abdomen.

The queen ants and the males are usually winged, with the other females of the nest, the worker ants (and those most commonly seen) being wingless. Occasionally, during the mating flights of the ants, tremendous numbers of winged males will be seen in swarms, and often these males will be blown onto the water. When this happens, the effect upon the fish is similar to that of a tremendous mayfly hatch. The water will literally boil as the fish feed on the struggling ants.

Ants live in colonies, with the number present depending upon the individual species, and ranging from a few dozen to several thousand. For the most part they nest in the ground, forming the characteristic anthills with which everyone is familiar, although some species nest in hollows in trees and rotten logs. Anyone who has had the misfortune to spread a picnic cloth over one of these hills knows amply well the numbers of ants that can be contained below ground!

The habits of ants are varied—some of them feed upon vegetable matter, some are strictly meat eaters, and others are scavengers, eating whatever happens to fall their way. For this reason, many households are plagued with the creatures, that will subsist upon crumbs, spilled sugar, and even virtually undetectable films of grease on ovens and cookware. Most of the species will bite when disturbed; however, the great majority are so small that little or no damage is done unless one is actually covered by the creatures.

The patterns that follow are divided into three major categories—Fur Ants, Hardshell Ants, and Flying Ants—and one specific pattern, the Velvet Ant, which accounts for the larger fish to be caught, such as bass.

I stress the point that no fly-fisherman can have too many ant patterns in his boxes. They cover the size range from the typical mayfly sizes down through those of the tiniest of midges. In addition, they may be tied in three standard colors, with or without wings, with the wings in various positions (erect or spent), and they may be fished either wet or dry. For all practical purposes, the ant is the most versatile pattern for all seasons to be obtained by the flytier-fisherman.

FUR ANTS

Since all ant patterns are tied in virtually the identical manner, we shall start with the most common imitations and give full tying instructions for these. The other major classes of patterns will explain the simple variations only, so whether or not the tier intends to tie the fur-bodied style, he should read this section for general construction details.

Hook: #'s 14–28, regular length.
Thread: Black, red, or tan.
Body: Black, rust, or cinnamon. Several materials may be used. Natural fur has the greatest translucency, but polypropylene dubbing is almost as effective and much easier to work with.
Legs: Black, brown, or ginger hackle.
Head: Black, red, or tan tying thread.

The tying thread should be half-hitched to the shank of the hook near the bend and waxed heavily with a good grade of tacky tying wax to cause good adhesion of the body material. The three colors of body material represent the three most common varieties of ant to be found, the black ant, the red ant, and the cinnamon ant.

While natural fur is undoubtedly the best material for these ants, because of its natural translucency in the water, dyed fur may be substituted if the natural shades are not readily available. Dyed furs tend to lose much of their natural oils and gloss in the dyeing process, and natural furs such as mink and otter, water-loving creatures, can be obtained in the required natural colors with a little perseverance. These furs are the best for the ant patterns, because their sheen looks almost precisely like the actual body of an ant in the water.

In the absence of furs, polypropylene dubbing materials may be used in the required colors, and are actually preferable to dyed furs. Any of the brands now on the market are excellent; one of the latest additions to the field is a material called Seal-X, developed by Poul Jorgensen as an effective substitute for seal fur on salmon flies and nymphs. This material not only spins better than seal fur, it has greater sheen and translucency than many of the other polypropylene materials.

Spin a very small pad of the body material onto the thread as close to the shank of the hook as possible, and spin it tightly. Now wrap a hump onto the shank, approximately one-third the length of the shank, and almost perfectly round. Tie it off with two half-hitches, and strip off whatever body material remains on the thread.

Now advance the thread forward another third of the length of the shank, half-hitch it, and tie in the hackle feather. Wrap the hackle two or three turns, depending upon the size of the fly, in the center of the thread-covered portion, so that there is definition between the rear hump and the rear of the hackle legs. Tie off the hackle and trim it.

Moving the thread forward again, spin another very small amount of dubbing material onto the thread and make another hump, slightly smaller than the first, between the forward edge of the hackle and the eye of the hook. Tie it off with a whip finish, and apply a drop of head cement to both the head windings and the base of the hackle fibers for durability. The resulting fly will look approximately like this:

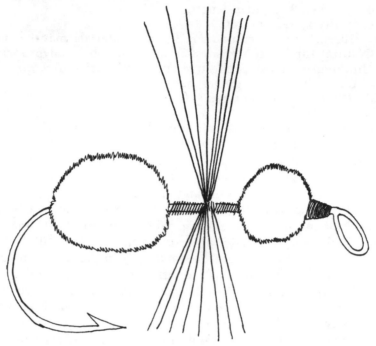

The black ant will be the largest encountered; for greatest effectiveness, I recommend eliminating the top two hook sizes (#'s 14 and 16) when tying the red and cinnamon ants. While this size differentiation is not crucial when angling for such hearty strikers as bluegills and other panfish, it does seem to make a difference on the trout stream.

HARDSHELL ANTS

There are many cases in which one requires a wet fly ant pattern. Although the Fur-Bodied Ant will sink if not treated with dry fly dope, there is a means of creating a fly that will sink more readily and quickly, an especially valuable commodity when fishing deep holes.

The Hardshell Ants can be made in two ways. The first, and most time-consuming, is to build up the body with regular tying thread. Use a thread of very fine diameter, such as monofilament nymph thread, in the proper colors, and build the two humps as smoothly as possible. Then, using very thin fly-tying cement or clear nailpolish, saturate each lump several times until the body is perfectly smooth and glossy.

There are those tiers who will inform the reader to use any thread and enamel the body to the desired color of the finished ant. While they have their reasons, I cannot recommend this process, for the simple reason that most enamels will chip. The clear lacquer or cement will penetrate the thread fully, and provide a clear aura about the fly to give it the appearance of translucence—one of the most important features in almost every insect imitation.

The second method of creating the wet ant involves the use of acetate floss. This marvelous creation builds up rapidly into a body of the proper size, so is far less time-consuming in that respect. In addition, since the acetone solution that dissolves the floss is harmless to thread or feathers, the entire fly may be tied and then dipped, complete, into the solution.

A word of warning, however. The acetone, while not affecting the materials themselves, *will* dissolve some types of head cement. If the acetate floss method is employed, do not cement the thread at the head until after the acetone has evaporated from the fly and the floss has set up. Simply half-hitch or whip finish the head, and leave a 2″ to 3″ length of thread attached. You can then hold onto the thread while dipping the fly into the acetone.

After dipping, wave the fly back and forth for thirty seconds, until the floss is set. Then apply a dab of cement to the head and cut the thread off flush with the head. The body is now solid plastic, and one of the most durable artificials you will have ever tied.

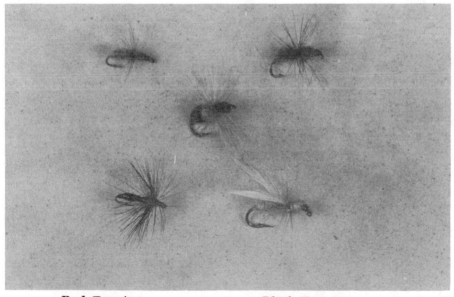

Red Fur Ant   Black Fur Ant
Velvet Ant
Black Hardshell Ant   Cinnamon Flying Ant

A point to note is that, while the acetate method is much easier and faster than the thread method, both in the tying and the strengthening, acetate floss itself is quite bulky. For this reason, it is not as effective as the thread in sizes 22 and smaller. The one advantage is that, when one reaches hooks of that size, regular tying thread will create the bodies in only slightly greater time than it takes to make the acetate bodies on the larger numbers.

Wet ants of all sizes, as in the case of fur ants, belong in the terrestrial fisherman's boxes. The extra time spent in whipping up some of the smaller sizes will be amply repaid in late summer, low-water situations.

FLYING ANTS

The additional tying instructions for the Flying Ants are quite simple. Pale blue dun hackle points (for the black ant) and ginger hackle points (for the red and cinnamon ants) are tied in between the two humps in the same manner as for standard dry flies. In addition, four or five turns of the hackle are used instead of two or three for the legs, since these flies need the extra buoyancy.

The wings may be added in any one of three styles: folded, spent, or erect, as shown by the illustration below:

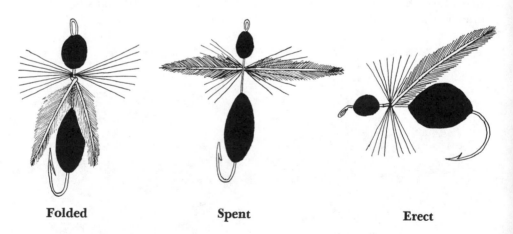

Folded **Spent** **Erect**

These flies are particularly effective when there is a large flight of males being blown onto the water. Either match the size of the naturals exactly, or go slightly larger. Smaller flies will be overlooked by the fish in their feeding frenzy on the naturals, but often a slightly larger fly will draw the fish away from a natural to the artificial sitting right beside it.

VELVET ANT

Strictly speaking, the velvet ant is not an ant at all, but a wasp of the family Mutillidae in which the female workers are wingless and look almost exactly like ants. They are larger than common ants, however, and extremely hairy. The females can give a severe sting. These are ground-living ants, found over much of the Eastern half of the United States, and the pattern is effective on largemouth bass as well as trout and panfish.

> Hook: #'s 6–8, regular length.
> Thread: Black.
> Abdomen: Polypropylene dubbing material in three bands—
> burnt orange at tail, then black, then burnt orange.
> Thorax: Burnt orange dubbing.
> Head: Burnt orange dubbing.
> Legs: Black hackle.

The Velvet Ant is tied in the same manner as the various bee and wasp patterns, save the fact that wings are absent. The most accurate representation of the true color of the velvet ant is to be found in Burnt Orange Seal-X, but any reddish orange poly dubbing materials may be used.

Again, pay particular attention to the separation of the various sections of the body.

When the fly is finished and the whip-finished head is cemented, take a bodkin or needle and pick out the abdomen and thorax to give a very fuzzy appearance.

Ants in general do not float high on the surface as do some of the aquatic insects with which most fly-fishermen have become familiar, so be sparing with the hackle, and with the dry fly spray. The live insects tend to float in, rather than on, the surface tension, and it is to the angler's advantage to try to duplicate this half-sodden float with the artificials.

11

LEAFHOPPERS

The trout were dimpling the water ahead of me so regularly that for a moment I checked to see if it was raining. It wasn't. In fact, it hadn't rained for seven weeks, and the slow, shallow stream was as clear as gin. Having fished for three hours without so much as a single rise, I was beginning to wish that the water was as alcoholic as it looked, just to give me some legitimate reason for being out there.

I stood in the middle of the stream and peered closely at the water to determine what the fish ahead of me were taking. I couldn't see a thing.

"Must be midges," I thought. "In fact, it has to be midges, since I don't have any with me."

Slowly, so as not to put down the fish, I worked my way toward the grassy bank, and, getting down on my hands and knees, began to crawl along the shore to a point opposite the feeding fish in the hopes of discovering the fly of the hour. And suddenly a cloud of something hit me in the face as it sailed toward the water's edge, and I heard the dimpling turn into a slurping and smacking. Forgetting the water's surface for a moment, I turned my attention to the grasses themselves. For a moment they looked barren, and then I saw them—small, pale insects, slightly larger than midges but, because of their delicate camouflage coloration, harder to see. I knew what I was working with then, and I remembered the box in my vest pocket that I had almost forgotten—a synthesis of reading, and experimentation, which as yet I had never had the opportunity to use.

Slowly I edged back to my previous location, and tied one of the flies onto my tippet. A few false casts, and I dropped the fly at the edge of the grass—and was fast to an eleven-inch brown. On that day,

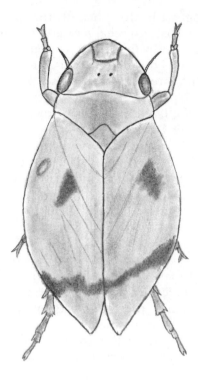

Leafhopper

which after three hours of futility provided a full hour of some of the fastest trout-fishing I have ever known, a love affair with the leafhopper was born.

The leafhopper has long been known to anglers under both that name and the term *jassid*. Technically speaking, these are small insects of the order Homoptera and two superfamilies—Cicadoidea and Fulgoroidea—comprised of fifteen separate families. For the most part, the differences in these families are such that only a trained entomologist would be able to distinguish between them, and in fact once the flytier has gotten the hang of tying the leafhoppers, any species can be effectively duplicated with the same general pattern, simply by altering the color.

Homoptera feed entirely on plants, and are sometimes present in such tremendous numbers that when disturbed they literally seem to swarm. The various species are quite selective, each choosing a particular part of a relatively few species of plants for its sustenance. Plants with a very heavy infestation generally do not survive, since the feeding activity causes damage in the form of wilting, discoloration, and stunting, and because of this many of the species are considered to be severe pests on cultivated plants. In addition to their destructive feeding activity, some of the species are vectors, or carriers, of various plant diseases.

The leafhoppers, along with the ants of the previous chapter and the thrips in the final pattern chapter, are the midges of the terrestrial world as far as the fly-fisherman is concerned. They are abundant, particularly in mid- to late summer when aquatic midges are off the water; and they are found in close proximity to most bodies of water. They are especially effective on trout, and will take many species of panfish as well, particularly in low, clear water situations where a very fine tippet is required.

I have discovered that the patterns developed by tiers before me cover the field, and so I shall give credit where credit is due to the men who developed these patterns. One of them I have had the good fortune to know; the others, only through their writings. Nonetheless, I feel I owe a debt of gratitude to all of them for developing terrestrial patterns that do not fail when the water is down and the midges aren't hatching.

There are eight patterns of leafhoppers, or jassids, that will be covered in this chapter and that, because of their different tints, cover the field admirably. Since these flies are used on very fine tippets for low water situations, and since they are frequently taken by surprisingly large fish, I strongly recommend carrying several of each pattern. There is nothing more frustrating than having a large rainbow take your last fly of a given pattern when the trout are boiling the water for that very insect.

JASSID

The pattern that follows was developed by one of the great innovators in fly tying, Vince Marinaro. It is one of the most effective Leafhopper, patterns available as a searching pattern, although some of the others to follow are closer imitations of the living insects.

> Hook: #'s 20–24, regular length, light wire.
> Body: Black tying silk.
> Legs: Short, black hackle, tied palmer the full length of the body and cut off beneath.
> Wing: Single junglecock eye (or substitute) tied flat along the back.

The hackle is wound fully and closely, as one would tie a standard bivisible. These hackles must be short, coming from the end of the cock neck closest to the head, since fine points (rather than the heavy, blunt points of clipped hackle) are necessary to the proper appearance of the fly. The legs should be trimmed flat on the bottom, not only to provide a proper float, but also to improve the hooking qualities of the very small hooks. With a #24 hook with palmered hackle, the stiff fibers along the bottom could easily fill the hook gap and prevent effective hooking.

The original pattern calls for natural junglecock, which can no longer be imported into this country. Some enterprising persons are now attempting to breed this bird in America, for the fly-tying fraternity. Until this happens, most of us are going to have to be satisfied with substitutes.

Starling feathers, taken from young birds, which have the white tip, are a very effective substitute, but any small feather will work if lacquered. I have used the plastic junglecock eyes now on the market, and although they are excellent substitutes for the real thing on the shoulders of salmon fly patterns, I cannot recommend them for the Jassid. Go to a small, natural feather, and you will be pleased with the result.

The following six patterns were all originated by one of the greatest flytiers and developers of all times, Bill Blades. The late Mr. Blades created some of the most realistic-looking artificials that the world had ever seen, and some of his nymph patterns, when the bend of the hook is concealed, cannot be readily distinguished from the living larvae.

For the most part the six patterns are self-explanatory. Where there may be any question, I have appended a few tying hints at the end of the list.

JASSID NO. 1

> Hook: #20, regular length, fine wire.
> Thread: Yellow.
> Body: Yellow raffia or latex sheet.
> Wings: Pale green duck wing quill.
> Legs: Yellow hackle.
> Head: Lacquer over yellow tying thread.

JASSID NO. 2

Hook: #20, regular length, fine wire.
Thread: Pale olive.
Body: Pale olive raffia or latex sheet.
Wings: Olive duck quill with two red fibers from a ringneck
    pheasant body feather on each side of the hook, angling
    slightly down.
Legs: Yellow hackle.
Head: Lacquer over olive tying thread.

JASSID NO. 3

Hook: #20, regular length, fine wire.
Thread: Tan.
Body: Tan raffia or latex sheet.
Wings: Woodcock or grouse body feather.
Legs: Yellow hackle.
Head: Lacquer over tan tying thread.

POTATO LEAFHOPPER

Hook: #22, regular length, fine wire.
Thread: Green.
Wings: Single section of green duck quill, soaked in rubber
    cement and folded over body.
Body: Green polypropylene dubbing.
Legs: Olive hackle.

ROSE LEAFHOPPER

Hook: #20, regular length, fine wire.
Thread: Primrose.
Wings: Single section of pale yellow duck quill, soaked in rubber
    cement and folded over body.
Body: Golden olive polypropylene dubbing.
Legs: Golden olive hackle.

LATERAL LEAFHOPPER

Hook: #22, regular length, fine wire.
Thread: Tan.
Wings: Woodcock or grouse body feather, soaked in rubber
    cement and folded over body.
Body: Golden brown polypropylene dubbing.
Legs: Fiery brown hackle.

In all cases, the original Blades patterns were tied with materials that were available to him at the time, and that, because of current import restrictions, are no longer obtainable. I have taken the liberty of substituting currently available materials, which retain the same color and texture. I have tied them with substitute materials for years, and have noticed no decline in effectiveness. In fact, the newer polypropylene dubbing materials are even more effective than Blades's original body materials, due to better translucency. These synthetic body material dubbings, particularly Poul Jorgensen's Seal-X, are not only readily obtainable through all of the major fly-tying materials sources, but just as effective as kapok as well as being a bit more durable.

In the numbered Jassid patterns, the feather is tied on in the same manner as the junglecock eye in the Marinaro Jassid, that is, flat along the top of the hook, like a flat wing case on nymphs. It should extend no farther than 1/16″ past the bend of the hook.

In the named patterns, the wings are tied caddis-style, that is, a single slip of wing quill is saturated with rubber cement and allowed to dry. Then it is trimmed as shown in the illustration below, and tied in when the head is formed with tying thread.

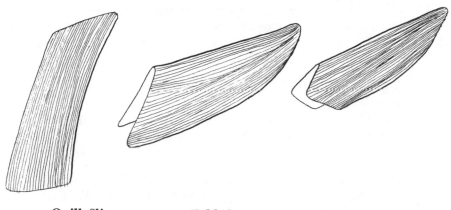

Quill Slip   **Folded**   **Trimmed**

For the first three patterns, the hackle should be tied palmer for the entire length of the hook. In the last three, the hackle should cover only the forward half of the hook. In all cases the hackle should be trimmed across the bottom to assure proper flotation and hooking qualities.

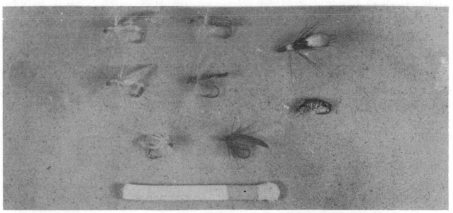

Jassid #3   Jassid #2   Marinaro Jassid
Jassid #1   Potato Leafhopper   Jorgensen Leafhopper
          Rose Leafhopper   Lateral Leafhopper

Blades recommended trimmed hackle stems for the legs, and I have taken the liberty of changing that recommendation to palmered hackle. The trimmed hackle stems of the original patterns certainly give a great realism to the patterns, but they are extremely difficult to tie in effectively, and quite time-consuming. Trimmed hackle stems may be used for display patterns, but are no more effective in the water than palmered hackle, so for the man who desires only fishing patterns, stick with the palmered hackle.

The following pattern is one of the most difficult to tie that you will find in this book, but for a high-floating leafhopper you will be hard put to find a more effective pattern. It was originated by Poul Jorgensen of Towson, Maryland, a professional tier who does beautiful work. The pattern is as follows:

Hook: #22, regular length, light wire.
Thread: White.
Body: Light gray caribou hair, spun as for a deer hair bug (see instructions in grasshopper section).
Wings: Fibers of grouse feather.

All the materials are easy to obtain, with the difficulty lying solely in the spinning of the caribou hair on such a small hook. The thread should be started at the *bend* of the hook (to provide free spinning for the hair), and six fibers from a grouse feather should be tied in by their tips, with the body of the fibers extending well past the bend of the hook.

The hair is then applied in the same manner as for the various deer hair patterns mentioned earlier in the book. Although Jorgensen specifies caribou hair, I recommend antelope hair if obtainable. It is a finer diameter hair, and spins more readily on a #22 hook, and it is easier to work with, if any hair spinning on such a hook can be called easy.

Once the hair is spun, draw the grouse feather fibers forward to the eye of the hook, making certain that they lie evenly over the back of the caribou (or antelope) body, which has been trimmed closely enough to provide hook gap clearance. Tie the fibers in at the head, and whip finish.

Jorgensen's fly will float without adding any treatment due to the hollow hairs, but, like all deer hair patterns, it will eventually soak up water. Depending upon the manner in which the naturals are floating, you may either treat the fly (for a high floater) or simply squeeze the excess water out of the hair and blow on it (for a pattern that will float in rather than on the surface tension).

I cannot stress too highly the importance of the various Leafhopper patterns to the fly fisherman's repertoire. From spring until fall, leafhoppers are in evidence—and that includes the hot, dry periods in late summer and early fall when there are no aquatic hatches on the water, and when the water is extremely low and crystal clear.

At these times, a very small fly on a very fine tippet is the only offering that will take trout. In gin-clear water, the trout cannot only see a heavy leader, but they can see precisely what the fly looks like, as well. In these situations, there is no mayfly or midge that is going to consistently take trout. Only the leafhoppers can entice them with any regularity, and for the trouter who gives up when August and September arrive, these patterns can be the key to an extra two months of fast and glorious fishing.

12

BEETLES

By this time the bass fisherman may have started feeling forgotten; the crickets and hoppers, and a few of the fly and bee patterns, are quite effective for bass, but most of the other patterns mentioned have been for selective trout and the smaller panfish (do not, however, be surprised if a largemouth nails a Velvet Ant or any of the landflies— it doesn't happen often enough to warrant using those patterns exclusively for bass, but many a bluegill trip has had the extra excitement of a two-pound largemouth heading for deep water with a ridiculously small fly buried past the barb in his jaw).

However, this chapter is designed for the angler who seeks bass particularly, as well as those budding Theodore Gordons who search for the lunker trout in deep, meadow streams and forgotten beaver ponds. Beetles are large, succulent insects, and so are drawing cards in that right; but they are effective for another reason—perhaps a more important one—as well.

The larger a fish grows, the less energy it wishes to expend in chasing its food. This is the reason that so many of the lunkers of all species are found so close to structure of various sorts, whether it be a sunken tree for a largemouth bass or an undercut bank fringed with roots for a large brown trout. These large fish lie in wait for whatever happens to venture too close to their lairs, and then make a short dash to take the creature in.

In short, the larger the fish, the slower the lure has to move; and the closer to the fish it has to be presented. Beetle imitations are perfect for this sort of terrestrial fishing, for when natural beetles land on the water they are often quite close to shore (and hence to the very structure we are seeking), and, although most beetles are relatively good swimmers, able to cross small lakes if necessary (and if not intercepted along the way), they are slow movers, twitching themselves along in the surface tension rather than skimming across it. The fly patterns should be dropped close to stumps, swept under overhanging trees, or allowed to drift with eddies under eroded banks, and twitched very slightly to give the appearance of a struggling insect. The strikes, when they come, are usually fast and violent.

Beetles are members of the order Coleoptera. They are characterized primarily by the fact that the forward wings (there are two pair) are thick, having the appearance or consistency of either chitin (like a crab shell) or leather. The rear wings are membranous as in other insects, but for the purpose of the flytier these wings are unimportant, since beetles that land on the water try to swim rather than fly, and hence the wings are folded, with the leathery wings folded over the membranous wings giving a very compact appearance. Beetles are readily identifiable from other insects, since they are hard bodied rather than soft bodied. Their larvae are quite variable in appearance; the Japanese beetle larva is the common white, red-headed grub often discovered while spading a lawn or garden.

Beetles comprise the largest order of insects in the world in relation to number of species. They feed upon all sorts of materials from plants to carrion and fecal material, and are found almost everywhere, in all climates and habitats.

Many of these beetles, and especially the Japanese beetle (not native to this country but far too well established), are quite serious crop pests, since there are beetles that feed on stems of plants, beetles that eat leaves of plants, and beetles that take their subsistence from the various fruits of crop plants—in short, given enough species in a given locale, entire plants can be destroyed. In addition, there are beetles (notably mealworms) whose larval and adult stages feed upon stored grain.

However, there are also species that are beneficial to man. The June bug beetles are extremely valuable since they consume other insects that are crop pests, and cultures of June bugs may be purchased through many gardening-supply houses. Dung beetles are valuable as scavengers, since they actually feed upon fecal material.

Although there are several species of aquatic beetles, they are generally covered in other texts, and are not the focal point of this chapter. In the first place, while it may seem reasonable that aquatic beetles would be effective, in point of fact they are not. There are very few species of aquatic beetles that are actively fed upon by fish, since in their adaptive evolution they have developed many features unattractive to fish—taste, toxins, or sharp spines discourage feeding. The only beetle commonly fed upon that makes its home in the water is the back-swimmer brown; this pattern is presented in this chapter for those who desire it, even though it is not a terrestrial. Nevertheless, the chapter on beetles would not be considered complete by many tiers without the back-swimmer. It is an additional, rather than a necessary, pattern.

The first two patterns offered are general beetle representations; these are the most important, since they rely upon general form and coloration rather than direct imitation. For the tier who only desires a few of the bulky beetles in his boxes, these are the essentials. The following two are imitations of the Japanese and June bug beetles. These are quite effective, and should definitely be added by anyone with the time and inclination to do so. The last pattern is the back-swimmer brown.

BLACK DEER HAIR BEETLE

This pattern was developed by Poul Jorgensen, and is quite effective whenever there are black beetles to be found on shore, in decaying logs, close to the water's edge. Created of deer hair, it floats quite well, especially since in the manner in which it is tied there are just a few open ends of deer hair to absorb water.

> Hook: #'s 8–20 (Mustad #94833).
> Body: Black tying thread wound over black deer hair.
> Wing Case: Black deer hair folded over body (see instructions below) and tied off at head.
> Legs: Butts of deer hair bent back from tying in body and trimmed to proportionate length.
> Head: Trimmed butts of the wing case hairs.

Actually, this is quite a simple pattern to tie, since the body is not spun in the manner common to deer hair bugs. Choose deer body hair that is three to four times the length of the hook shank. Approximately eight hairs are the proper number for a #20 hook. Add four to six hairs for each size larger hook. After a few flies you will be able to estimate the proper amount without counting.

Tie in the tying thread, and wrap a smooth double layer underlay, ending up approximately 3/16 to 1/16″ behind the eye of the hook (depending upon the size of the hook). Now tie in the bunch of deer hair, letting the butts extend half the length of the hook shank past the eye. Wind the thread tightly to the bend of the hook, and tie with three half-hitches. Now wind the thread back to where it was originally tied in.

Bend back three of the hairs on each side that extend past the eye, and wind the thread in front of them so that they remain extended to the sides.

Now grasp the tips of the hairs that extend past the bend of the hook and pull them forward over the eye, keeping them along the

Japanese Beetle   June Bug Beetle
Brown Beetle   Black Beetle

back of the fly. Tie them off, making certain that they remain on top of the fly body, and half-hitch several times.

All that remains now is to pull the three hair butts on either side of the fly apart so that they simulate the legs of the beetle, and to trim the hairs that extend past the eye of the fly to a proportionate length to the length of the hook to form the head. The Black Deer Hair Beetle is then finished.

For the purists, Jorgensen recommends a coat of vinyl cement for the fly. I personally do not use it, for the cement adds weight and therefore makes the fly float lower in the water. Admittedly, an untreated fly will not last as long, but I have caught eleven bass on a #8 beetle before the hairs started giving way, and any time I can take that many bass before a fly *starts* to unravel, I am more than satisfied with ten minutes at the bench.

BROWN BEETLE

This is my own pattern, similar to Jorgensen's Black Beetle in materials but tied in a slightly different manner, and representative of the many beetles of brown to green hue that are found periodically upon the water. For the tier only interested in the two essential patterns, this beetle will take care of the Japanese Beetles in size 8, as well as many other species of beetles in the smaller sizes.

Hook: #'s 8–14, (Mustad #94833).

103

Thread: Brown.
Body: Brown to gray deer hair, spun in bass bug fashion.
Wing case: Brown bucktail.
Legs: Moose mane.
Head: Brown tying thread.

Tie in the thread at the bend of the hook. Then tie in a small bunch of brown bucktail by the butts, winding the thread over the butts to make a smooth finish. Now spin on the brown deer hair in the manner described for the various deer hair hoppers.

Bring the bucktail over the back of the beetle as described for the Black Deer Hair Beetle, and tie off just behind the eye of the hook. Now take three long strands of moose mane, and lay them across the back of the fly, ⅓ of the way back from the eye. Tie a loop of another length of tying thread over these hairs, cinching it enough to provide a segmentation to the body. Now bind in the moose mane, winding the threads between the individual hairs to separate them. Trim the hairs to proportionate length, trim the bucktail extending over the eye of the hook to provide the head (as in the Jorgensen pattern), and lacquer all the windings. Because of the buoyancy of this fly, the bucktail back may be lacquered in order to provide durability.

JAPANESE BEETLE

While the Brown Beetle is a good general pattern when unidentified beetles of that hue are on the water, the Japanese Beetle pattern is more effective in mid- to late summer when the real Japanese beetles are committing their depredations throughout the countryside, especially in farm ponds, which are very likely to have these actual beetles floating upon the surface.

Hook: #'s 8–10.
Thread: Brown.
Body: Coarse tan chenille, saturated with rubber cement and pressed to flatten into an oval.
Wing case: Brown pheasant body feather, lacquered.
Legs: Mottled pheasant body feather, lacquered and shaped.
Head: Brown tying thread.

The thread is tied in at the bend of the hook and wrapped to ⅛" behind the eye, and back to the bend again. A mottled brown pheasant body feather is then coated with rubber cement, and shaped as shown on page 105.

This feather is tied in by the tip at the bend of the hook, extending toward the tail of the fly. A length of coarse chenille is then tied in

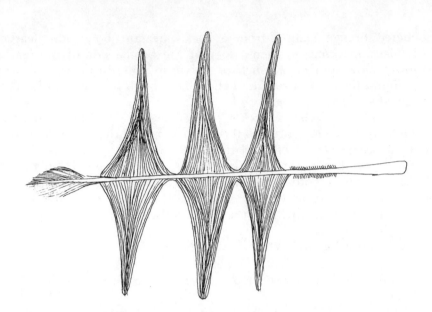

and wrapped to 1/8" behind the eye of the hook and back again. Tie it off, soak the chenille with rubber cement, and, when it begins to get tacky, compress it with either your fingers or flat-jawed pliers to provide a flat, oval body. Now pull the pheasant feather forward and tie it off behind the eye of the hook. Tie in a lacquered brown feather by the butt, letting it extend to the bend of the hook. If the feather tends to cock a little into the air, a drop of cement between the wing case and the lacquered feather forming the legs will hold it in place.

Wrap a medium head with the tying thread, whip finish it, and coat the head liberally with cement. The fly sounds complicated, but if the feathers for the legs and wing case are made up in advance they can be stored until needed. The most time-consuming part of the whole fly is waiting for the various cements to dry.

JUNE BUG BEETLE

The June Bug Beetle is a small beetle pattern, quite effective on both trout and panfish. It is a simple little fly to tie, and worth adding to the boxes of ants and leafhoppers as a searching pattern.

    Hook: #'s 14–20.
    Thread: Orange.
    Body: Rusty orange polypropylene dubbing.
    Legs: Black hackle.
    Wing case: Mottled orange pheasant body feather.
    Head: Orange tying thread.

Start the thread at the bend of the hook, and tie in the tip of a lacquered orange feather from a cock pheasant body—the feathers with black markings to them—so that the bright side of the feather is down. Now spin on a pinch of polypropylene dubbing, and wrap a medium-thick body from the bend of the hook for two thirds of the length of the shank.

Tie in a *small* black hackle feather by its tip directly in front of the body, and wrap it two to three times around the hook, depending upon hook size. Tie it off, and trim the butt.

Finally, pull the pheasant feather forward, keeping it on the top of the hook, over both body and hackle, and tie it off, trimming the butt and wrapping and whip finishing the head. Give the head a coat of fly-tying cement, and the fly is finished.

BACK-SWIMMER BROWN

This Back-Swimmer Brown pattern is not to be confused with the

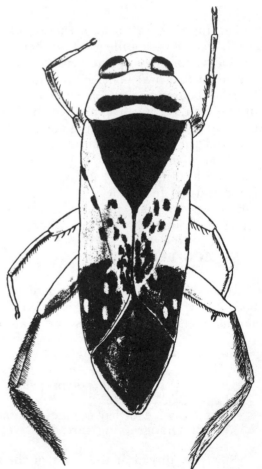

Backswimmer Brown

relatively common nymph pattern of the same name. It is a misnomer for the nymph, and a very descriptive term for the small water beetle otherwise known as a water boatman. Back-swimmers, of the family Notonectidae, are very common in ponds, and take their names from the fact that they swim upside down, stroking across the surface with powerful strokes of their hind legs, which have evolved like oars.

Not truly a terrestrial, and not as effective a searching pattern as the other beetles mentioned above, this pattern is included because it is one of the most commonly tied of all the beetle patterns. It also makes a nice display pattern because of the construction of the legs, which are difficult to tie but very natural looking and effective both on the water and in a display case.

Hook: #'s 6–8, 2X long.
Thread: Fiery brown.
Body: Fiery brown (golden brown) polypropylene dubbing.
Legs: Knotted hackle stems, with the fibers left on the ends of the rear legs.
Wing case: Brown latex, stippled with magic marker.
Head: Fiery brown tying thread.

This pattern differs from most other patterns in that the legs are tied in first to give them their proper location in the finished fly. Choose two narrow brown hackles, approximately twice the length of the hook shank (some will be trimmed off later in tying). Now strip off all the fibers except those along the tip of the hackle. Soak the feathers in warm water to make them supple, and tie a knot in the stem where the fibers end.

Lay these stripped and knotted hackle stems across the hook as shown in the illustration, tie them off with figure-eight wraps, and trim away the butts. Now take two more hackles, *completely* strip away all the fibers, and tie them to the shank of the hook in the shape of a cross. The fly should now look like this:

Trim the ends of the hackle forelegs to even them up, and wind the thread back to the bend of the hook. Tie in a strip of light brown latex, $1/4''$ wide by $1''$ long, and half-hitch it securely. Now spin a generous quantity of polypropylene dubbing onto the thread, and wind a full body, working right up against the rear legs, figure-eighted between them, and between the two pairs of forelegs. This keeps the forelegs separated, and helps to hold all the legs in place, as well as strengthening the tie by, in effect, double-wrapping the leg ties. Wind the dubbing all the way to the eye of the hook, and tie it off.

Now grab the latex strip and stretch it forward over the back of the fly, so that it stretches part of the way down the sides of the Back-swimmer and conforms to the shape of the body. Tie it off approximately $1/16''$ behind the eye, trim away the excess, and wrap a smoothly covered head with the tying thread. Whip finish the head, and coat fully and smoothly with thinned fly-tying cement.

The markings on the back of the Back-swimmer are applied with magic markers. Be certain that the type you use are waterproof if you intend to use this fly; some of them aren't, and there is nothing more frustrating than to spend all the time required creating a very lifelike fly only to find the dark brown mottlings washed away after the first few casts. The drawing of the back-swimmer will provide a guide for the markings.

13

SOWBUGS AND OTHERS

In wrapping up the pattern section of *Tying and Fishing the Terrestrials*, we find ourselves left with a few patterns that, although quite important for the full range of fly-rod use, are not as well known to the fly-fisherman as some of the other terrestrials. These patterns include sowbugs, cress bugs, cockroaches, and thrips and psyllids, which make up the midge area of the terrestrial fisherman's repertoire.

These are all very simple patterns to tie; in fact, their simplicity and effectiveness are such that it is surprising that they are not mentioned in more fly-tying tomes. To my knowledge, only the sowbug and the cress bug have even been mentioned, and these have not been given the coverage or explanation necessary to their effective use, with the exception of Ed Koch's Cress Bug pattern in his excellent book, *Fishing the Midge*.

I personally believe that these oddments in the terrestrial fisherman's repertoire are essential patterns. They are insects and, in the case of the sowbug, insect relatives that are seldom noticed, since their habits or small size do not place them as much in the angler's eye as do the habits and size of the leaping or flying insects mentioned in the other pattern chapters. These are definitely patterns to use when there is no insect life in evidence, either on or around the water, since these are creatures that fall into the water only sporadically, and fish are used to taking singles.

SOWBUG

To the best of my knowledge, the sowbug has been mentioned in only one other book on fly imitation, Ernie Schwiebert's comprehensive,

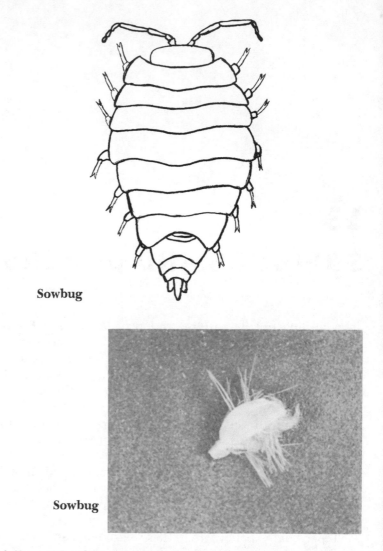

Sowbug

Sowbug

if difficult to follow, *Matching the Hatch*. The sowbug is not a true insect, but rather a close relative, a landbound crustacean of the class Isopoda, more closely related to the crab than to the insect. They are commonly found under rocks and beneath the bark of decaying logs near the water, and possess seven pairs of appendages, or legs.

Schwiebert's imitation is only a general representation of the arthropod, and not as effective on the water as the pattern that follows.

    Hook: #10.
    Thread: Gray nymph thread.
    Body: Medium gray chenille, trimmed top and bottom.
    Legs: Iron blue dun hackle tied palmer.
    Back: Dark gray latex, ribbed with tying thread.

The first step is to trim a piece of latex into the shape of the back of the insect, as shown below:

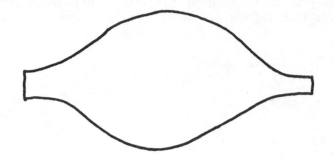

Starting at the bend of the hook, attach the tying thread and tie in a six-inch length of gray thread, a four-inch piece of medium-gray chenille, an iron-blue dun hackle feather, and one end of the piece of latex. Bring the main thread forward to the eye of the hook. Wrap the chenille around the shank to form an egg-shaped body, tie it off, and, with your scissors, trim the top and bottom of the chenille to form a flattened, oval body. Wind the hackle, palmer style, forward to the eye and tie it off. Stretch the latex back over the fly, keeping it on top as you did for the back-swimmer, and tie it in at the eye of the hook. Now rib the entire fly evenly with the loose piece of thread, and wrap off the head, ending with a whip finish and head cement. This fly looks like the real insect, and will float for some time on the water before drifting slowly to the bottom, just as the real arthropod behaves in the water.

CRESS BUG

There are two patterns of cress bugs, one developed by Ed Koch, and the other by Poul Jorgensen. Both are highly effective around beds of watercress (hence the name), lily pads, and thick growths of Elodea, duckweed, and moss.

The Jorgensen pattern is the simplest, so we will begin with that one.

Hook: #'s 8–20.
Thread: Brown.
Body: Medium olive spun fur, trimmed top and bottom.

Start the thread just behind the eye of the hook and wind back to the bend. Half-hitch the thread, and form a loop about four inches long, half-hitching the thread back at the bend and taking it forward to the eye.

Now choose a swatch of olive fur, muskrat preferably, and place it between the threads of the loop, spreading it out so that it looks like illustration A, below. Holding the thread loop taut, start twisting so that the thread traps the fur and spins it around, making a fur chenille.

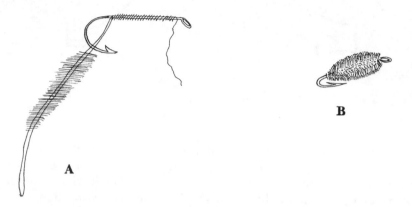

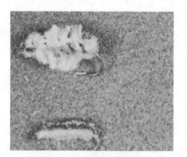

Now wind the fur chenille forward to the eye and tie it off with a whip finish. With your scissors, trim the top and bottom of the fly flat, and barber the sides into an oval, as shown in illustration B, above. Apply head cement to the winding, and the fly is complete.

Jorgensen Cress Bug
Koch Cress Bug

The Ed Koch Cress Bug is a little more complicated to tie, but it is still one of the simpler flies in the book.

Hook: #'s 16–22.
Thread: Gray.
Back Vein: Black ostrich or peacock herl.
Body: Gray foam rubber.
Head: Gray tying thread.

Attach the thread at the bend of the hook, and tie in two pieces of ostrich herl (preferred) or peacock herl. (The longer the fibers are on the herl, the better the fly will be in the water.) Attach a strip of gray foam rubber, ¼″ wide by approximately 1/64 to 1/32″ thick (available in most craft and hobby stores as well as millinery shops), and form a tapered body extending all the way to the eye of the hook. Tie off the foam and trim away the excess.

The herl is *not* palmered around the body, but instead is simply pulled forward across the back, keeping both herls atop the fly, and tied in behind the eye. The excess herl is then wrapped once or twice around the hook (depending upon the size), tied off with a whip finish.

COCKROACH

Cockroaches, of the order Orthoptera, family Blattidae, are one of the more common insect pests. They are also among the larger insects common to the United States, and hence are extremely attractive to lunker trout and bass. The most widely distributed cockroaches are those which invade homes and feed upon crumbs, garbage, and other food leavings. Cockroaches are insects of the dark, feeding at night and hiding in cracks and crevices during the day. They seldom fly, preferring to run instead, and are extremely fast. In addition to their other obnoxious characteristics, cockroaches also give off an unpleasant odor.

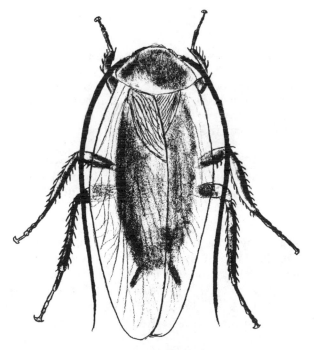

Wood Cockroach

113

There are, however, cockroaches found in the more northern states (from about the Mason-Dixon line north) that prefer life out of doors, and are found, like sowbugs, under rocks and beneath the bark of decaying logs. They occasionally fall into the water in their pursuit of food, and, in my personal experience, seldom if ever get back to shore.

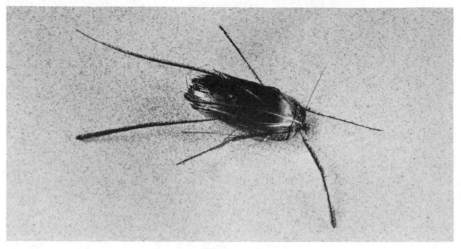

Cockroach

Hook: #2, 3X long.
Thread: Dark brown.
Body: Balsa wood, trimmed to shape, slotted to receive hook and legs, and painted brown.
Legs: Knotted peacock herl, set in cement.
Wings: Large crow body feather, lacquered and cemented to top of body.
Head: Painted markings on body and wing.

Cut an oval of 1/4" balsa wood to the shape shown below, and, with a razor blade, X-acto knife, or fine-bladed dovetail saw, make 1/16" deep cuts in top and bottom as shown in the illustration:

Wrap the shank of the hook with tying thread, and saturate it with epoxy cement. Remove the hook from the vise and insert the shank into the slot in the bottom of the body, with the body lying on its back. Block up the hook and let it dry undisturbed for twenty-four hours.

Place the hook back in the vise, fill the slots in the back of the fly with Duco cement, and insert the peacock herls as shown below:

Now paint the body with fast-drying brown model airplane dope,

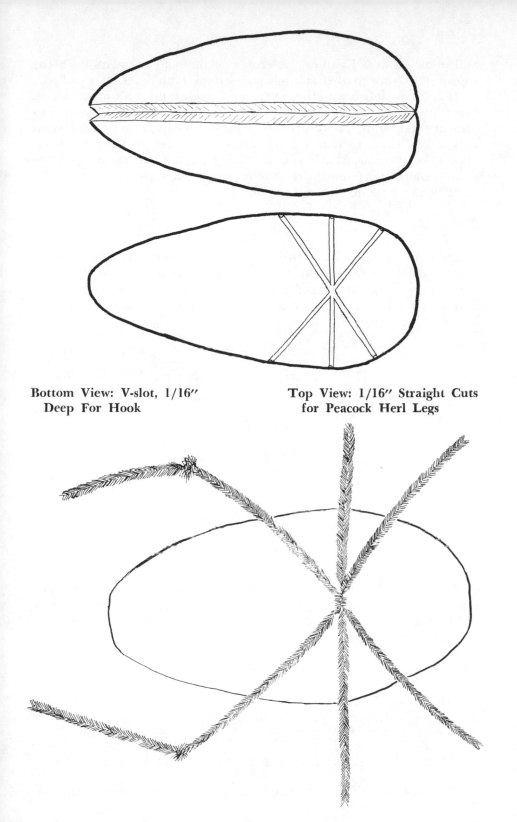

**Bottom View: V-slot, 1/16″
Deep For Hook**

**Top View: 1/16″ Straight Cuts
for Peacock Herl Legs**

and allow to dry. Lacquer the crow's feather, and cement it to the top of the body so that it slightly overlaps both sides of the body.

The fly is time-consuming to tie (although there isn't much actual tying involved) mainly because of the long drying times of the various cements and paint. However, each stage can be performed on several flies at one time, so that a good selection can be made without too great a loss of time. While you're waiting for the various components to dry, there are, after all, over four dozen other patterns and variations in the book to help fill up the time.

PSYLLIDS

Psyllids are one of the two true midge patterns available to the terrestrial tier. They should definitely be added to any box of terrestrials, since they will take fish often in the midst of aquatic midge hatches, and are superb flies for early morning and late evening in late summer, when the water is low and clear.

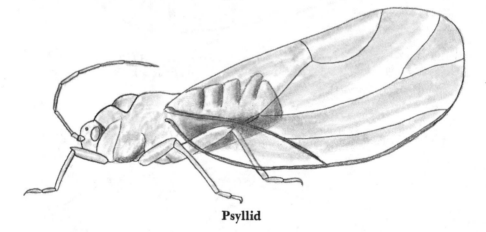

Psyllid

Most of the members of this family are nonparasitic, feeding upon a great variety of plants. Some of them form galls, that is, swellings on the leaves and stems of plants, in which the larvae, shaped like tiny, flattened grubs, are raised.

Psyllids have very short bodies, and oversized wings; a few species resemble miniature cicadas, to which they are related.

Hook: #'s 20–26.
Thread: Yellow nymph thread.
Body: Yellow nymph thread.
Legs: Cream hackle.
Wings: Pale ginger hackle, sized for a hook two sizes larger.

The body is built up of nymph thread, its diameter equalling one third its length. The wings are tied on directly behind the eye, tentlike over the body, and two turns of hackle (very short) are added on top of the wing butts. The head is then formed to the same diameter as the body, and whip finished. Although it is a very simple pattern, the small size of the hooks makes it difficult to get the wings to set properly at first. A little practice makes the process easier, and the fly is well worth the trouble.

THRIPS

Thrips comprise the order Thysanoptera, and are slender, quite small, and darkish in coloration. The wings are long and narrow, and the only insect wings that hackle feathers duplicate exactly since the actual wings are fringed with long, filamentous hairs.

Hook: #20.
Thread: Olive nymph thread.
Abdomen: Olive hackle quill, tied to extend past the bend of the hook.

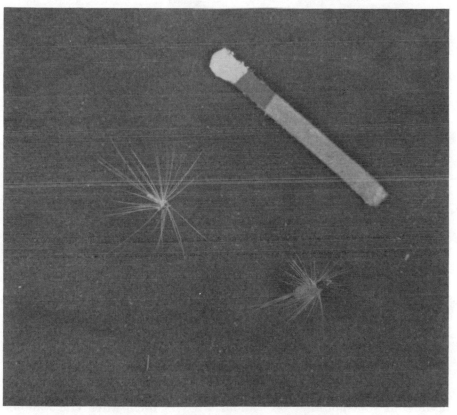

Psyllid   **Thrip**

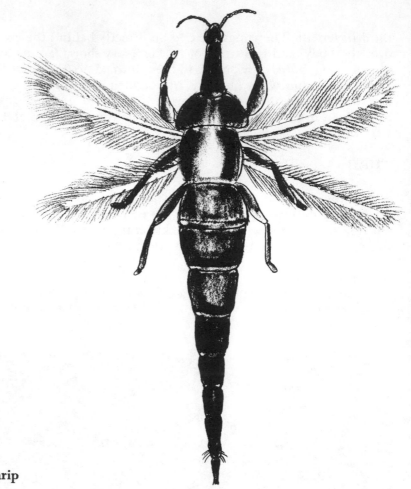

Thrip

Thorax: Olive polypropylene dubbing.
Wings: Four tiny pale blue dun hackle tips.

Start the tying thread at the eye of the hook, and bind in the stripped hackle quill so that it extends ¼″ past the bend of the hook. Spin a small bunch of olive poly dubbing material onto the thread, and cover the forward half of the hook shank and quill with the dubbing. Now tie in the hackle tips. This is a very difficult process, and it helps considerably to place a drop of thickened cement on top of the fly and hold the butts of the wings in the cement until they will stay on their own without support; then tie in the normal manner.

Whip finish the head, and with a bodkin, pick out the thorax dubbing on the underside to simulate the short legs common to thrips.

Again, because of the size, this is a difficult pattern to tie; you won't plop down at the bench and turn out a dozen of these in an hour—but you shouldn't be without a few of them when late summer calls for miniature flies.

14

TERRESTRIAL TACKLE

This chapter is not designed to be the last word in fly-fishing equipment; there are many fly-fishing tools on the market that have their place in the fly-fisherman's repertoire; this chapter is designed solely for the terrestrial fisherman, (although many of the various forms of equipment recommended here may also be used for other forms of fly-fishing).

The recommendations given here are based upon two years experience in fishing the various terrestrial patterns offered in the preceding chapters, in the pursuit of the various species of fish mentioned in the chapters to follow. Because of the individuality of various fly-fishermen, as to both equipment preference and their own size and strength, I am certain that I will differ with a few anglers who have been on the water a while. Nevertheless, this chapter is designed for the angler just beginning with terrestrials, who has not yet developed personal preferences, and who needs a guide to the most generally practical equipment for this sort of fishing.

RODS

The rod is the most important piece of equipment for the fly-fisherman. Its length and stiffness determine the ease with which the line can be cast, its weight determines how tiring it will be after a few hours' casting, and its composition determines the characteristics that the individual rod will possess.

Today's fly rods are made of three basic materials: fiberglass, bamboo, and the newest entry into the field, graphite. Each of the different materials has its own advantages and disadvantages, so we shall be treating each as a separate entity.

Bamboo, or cane, fly rods are the oldest, and the traditional fly-fisherman's weapon. There is much to recommend them—they provide a more delicate presentation than the other varieties of rods, they are exceptionally beautiful to look at, and they possess a feel that man-made material has yet to duplicate. On the other side of the coin, they tend to be rather fragile, especially in the tip section. If they are not stored perfectly straight, they will "take a set"—that is, the cane will take on a permanent bend that will completely destroy the action of the rod. The better rods now can fight even the largest fish safely without taking a set, but the cheaper ones will sometimes take a set during a protracted battle with a large fish. They also require more care in the form of cleaning and treatment than the various synthetic rods, and the varnish must be kept even and smooth, in order to prevent any bare wood from soaking up moisture and separating at the glue joints. In addition, a fly-fisherman can purchase a battery of fiberglass rods, in all lengths and weights and actions, for the price of a single, really good split bamboo rod. However, in spite of the many disadvantages, if the angler has the money for the initial purchase, and the time and inclination to take care of the rod, he cannot go wrong with bamboo.

For the all-around fly-fisherman, the development of fiberglass as a rod material was a definite blessing. The synthetic provided rods with excellent action at a price that anyone could afford. Fiberglass fly rods are strong enough to land some of the larger saltwater fish, not to mention *anything* that can be taken on terrestrial imitations. They come in every length, action, weight, and color imaginable, and range in price from about ten dollars to well over one hundred dollars— however, don't necessarily assume that a one-hundred-dollar rod is going to be far superior to a twenty-dollar rod, especially if both are made by the same manufacturer. In many instances they use exactly the same blanks for all of their rods, the difference in cost relating to the finish on the rod and the fixtures employed—that is, guides, tip top, reel seat, handle, and windings. If you fish hard and long, it may be to your advantage to purchase one of the more expensive rods with carboloy guides and other special fittings, but for the weekend/ vacation-only fly-fisherman, such additions would be a definitely un-necessary expense.

The only really important factor in the choice of a fiberglass rod is action. Too many of the less expensive rods by small manufacturers have what members of the trade used to call "store action"; that is, the rod has a very soft action that swishes around nicely when a potential purchaser takes it off the rack and waves it back and forth. Soft actions only look effective; in practice, they don't deliver the line and fly properly, sometimes not even turning the leader over, and in addition they are extremely tiring to use, since they flex almost all the way down to the handle, putting unnecessary leverage against the casting arm. They will not set the hook properly, either—reflex action will cause the tip to dip when it is raised quickly, causing slack in the line when it should become immediately taut. They don't have the backbone to sink a large hook into a tough bass's mouth, either.

The proper action for a fly rod for terrestrial fishing is stiff, with a fast tip and with the power extending well into the butt. This action can be found in many reasonably priced fiberglass rods, and in almost all of the latest addition to the field, the graphite rod. Graphite rods are lighter than fiberglass, and therefore not as tiring to use over a day's solid fishing. They are very fast rods, having superb recovery and very little reflex dip. They provide the most delicate presentation available in a synthetic fiber rod, in addition to the power necessary for long casts and wrestling with lunker trout and bass.

Still, the graphite rod is a newcomer, and in spite of its obvious advantages it is still in the experimental stage. It appears to be more fragile than comparable fiberglass rods, although in normal use and with proper care this shouldn't prove too great a hindrance. Nevertheless, for most fly-fisherman the price range of the new graphites puts them out of range, since we once again, as with the good bamboo rods, are talking about one hundred dollars or more. It is to be hoped that with greater production and more experimentation, the price of graphite rods—a product of space-age technology, made of the same materials used in certain components of space vehicles—will come down to a more readily affordable level. At the present time, given a hundred

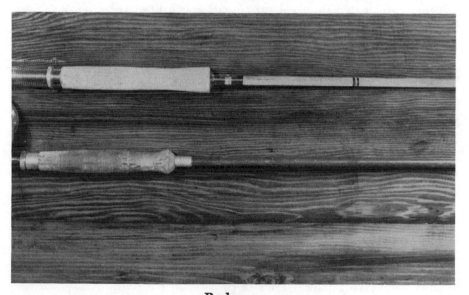

Rods

Bamboo
Fiberglass

bucks to spend on a fly rod, I would without hesitation choose a good bamboo.

Once you get past the various materials, and the action that you want, the only choice remaining is length, and here again the issue can become confusing. Fly rods range from ten- to twelve-foot monsters for saltwater fishing down to five-foot "midge" rods, covering almost every possible length in between. For the fish available to the terrestrial fisherman, 8½' is an ideal compromise length for a single rod. Such a rod has the delicacy of presentation for small flies in low water situations on trout, has the backbone for casting larger flies and wrestling largemouth bass out of lily pads, and is still light enough to give quite a bit of pleasure with panfish.

In recent years there has been quite a bit of interest shown in the shorter rods, called "midge rods" by the trade. They are supposedly more effective in presenting tiny flies in low water situations and, according to some self-proclaimed experts, provide more sport in a battle with smaller fish. Since the terrestrial fisherman, when employing the leafhoppers, psyllids, thrips, and small ants, may feel tempted to employ one of these short rods on the basis of what other writers have said, I offer these few comments so that the angler will be able to weigh the pros and cons for himself rather than taking any single authority's view.

As you will have gathered by now from my tone, I am not in favor of the short rods. With them, you are limited to very short casts (long-trained experts can work out a sizable amount of line with these rods, but the point is that the weekend/vacationer fisherman *cannot*) . There is nothing wrong with short casts—in fact, many of your casts will be short—but you should have the ability to lay out forty yards of line as effortlessly as you lay out twenty should a fish start feeding that far away.

A midge rod is certainly a lot of fun on panfish and small trout— but should a lunker inhale the fly, the midge rod hasn't got the backbone or the leverage to get the fish into the angler quickly. If you intend to take the fish home to eat, this isn't quite so important; however, more and more of our anglers are realizing the common sense in releasing fish to be enjoyed by someone else another day. Scientists have proved conclusively that the longer a fish has to fight against the rod, the greater the panic reaction that builds in its nervous system. This panic reaction causes the production of lactic acid, which builds up in the body tissues. Given a long fight, even if the fish is released, the buildup of this acid will cause its death in anywhere from a few minutes to a few days—and a dead fish that isn't sitting in someone's frying pan is a waste of a beautiful natural resource.

Midge rods do have their place—on small, heavily forested streams, where a longer rod would strike the foliage. Otherwise, the 8½' rod, with the proper choice of line and leader, will handle all of the flies, not to mention all of the fish, mentioned in this book in an effective, as well as very enjoyable, maner.

REELS

Basically—and this has been said so many times before that you should have it memorized by now—the fly reel is little more than a storage place for the line. As true as this is, there are certain features to look for in a reel, features that, in spite of the simple nature of the reel, make an important difference between the cheaper reels and the medium to expensive reels.

The first is line capacity. With the exception of lunker bass and huge brown or rainbow trout, you may never see the knot between your fly line and the backing. Nevertheless, if you do fish for the big ones occasionally, you should have a reel that will carry—without jamming—thirty-five yards of fly line plus at least fifty yards of twenty-pound test backing. Many anglers carry one hundred yards of backing, and certainly if you pursue only the largest fish, you should do so as well; however, be advised that the increased size of the reel necessary to contain the extra backing, plus the extra backing itself, is going to add weight to the outfit, and will require a correspondingly heavier rod to balance properly. Such a combination can become very fatiguing after only a few hours on the stream or lake.

Another feature quite valuable in reels is the availability of interchangeable spools. This, certainly, is only a convenience item, but

Various Fly Reels
(Automatic at Center Top)

much can be said for the convenience of being able to snap in a spool with lighter line, instead of having to strip off 105 feet of expensive coated line into the dirt, coil it properly, find some place to store it where it won't become damaged, tie on the new line and wind it evenly, set up a new leader, and start fishing again. Many feeding sprees simply don't last that long. And, while reels with interchangeable spools are frequently in the medium price range to expensive, the spools themselves are far less expensive than extra reels.

Look for a reel with some sort of drag; even the cheapest reels have click-antireverses, but these wear and are never really effective in slowing the run of a good fish. They also sound like a trash compacter. The best drag is a silent one, bearing evenly on the side of the spool, and adjustable to take care of the different tests of tippet used for different fish and under varying water conditions.

Fly reels come in two basic types—conventional and automatic. There are also a few very expensive multiplying reels on the market that may be of interest to the lunker bass fisherman, but for best all-around use the two basic types are the ones of greatest interest.

The conventional reel is the tried and true line container; due to the fact that the handle is often just a small, smooth plastic nubbin (even on the more expensive reels), it is virtually impossible to fight the fish from the reel as in the case of the various multiplying baitcasting or spinning reels on the market. The line must be stripped in, with the hands doing all the work of retrieving line and fighting the fish.

In the case of the automatic reel, there is no handle at all; a spring winds the spool, and a lever releases the spring to take up slack line. These reels still cannot be used to play fish, but have the advantage of keeping slack line on the reel rather than floating in the water or lying in the bottom of the boat. Because of this feature, if a fish should decide to run after some of the line has been retrieved, the fisherman will not discover—too late—that the line has looped around his leg, a protruding stump, or an oarlock, stopping the flow of the line abruptly and snapping the tippet.

On the other hand, there is more to go wrong with an automatic reel, and should the spring break or something jam, there is no way to manually return the line to the reel spool. They are also more expensive than many of the excellent medium-priced conventional fly reels (also called single-action reels), and considerably heavier in any given line capacity. Since most single-action reels have perforated spools to promote line drying, while automatics do not, for best performance the line should be stripped from the automatic at the end of each fishing day and allowed to dry—a tedious bit of work not necessary with conventional fly reels.

There you have it, quite briefly. Again, before purchasing *any* piece of tackle I recommend that you read one or more of the books listed in the Bibliography that deals at great length with fly-fishing equipment and techniques. For terrestrial fishing, my personal preference runs to a single-action, conventional fly reel, with a capacity of thirty-five yards of #7 weight line, and fifty yards of twenty-pound test braided nylon backing. I have never had a fish take all of the backing, and only a very few—all bass in the five- to eight-pound category, taken in open water—even reached the backing.

FLY LINES

Before getting into lines, I wish to clarify a point that I made in the above section in regard to backing. Many experts will recommend the use of monofilament as backing line. They have their reasons— notably, that monofilament has a smaller diameter for its pound test, and that all the quality that is necessary for backing that is seldom seen, much less actually used, can be obtained on bulk spools of several thousand yards for less than the cost of one hundred yards of "good" line. I'm not saying that they are wrong, but my personal preference runs to the braided nylon for two main reasons: first, it is softer, and lashes more easily to the butt of a fly line for a smooth joint that passes easily through the small snake guides; second, it does not have the "memory" of monofilament, and hence will not retain tight coils on the water if it should be needed—coils that have a horrid tendency, when stripped in, to spring a half-hitch around the rod tip. Those half-hitches can be disastrous when an eight-pound largemouth decides he wants another try at the hundred-meter run—both to the chances of ever landing the fish, and to the fine tip of the rod as well.

On the subject of fly lines themselves, much has been written on the subject, and a full discussion of the various weights and measurements can be found in several of the books mentioned in the Bibliography. For those not really wishing to understand all of the ramifications of line weights and tapers, the following guidelines will help you match a good line to your terrestrial outfit, so that you can get out there and have some fun without worrying about technicalities— most of which really have no bearing on the enjoyment of the fishing, anyway.

The only important factor for the beginning fly-fisherman to consider in the purchase of a fly line is that the first line he buys is weight-matched to his rod. As he progresses, he will be able to use heavier or lighter lines effectively, simply by altering his timing slightly in the cast, but to attempt to learn to cast with an unbalanced combination is folly. Fly-casting is no esoteric art—anyone can do it with a few hours' practice in the backyard—but it shouldn't be *made* difficult through the use of improper equipment.

It is easy to get the proper balance, since all lines are marked with their weight—e.g., WF-8-F (meaning weight-forward taper, weight

eight, floating line)—and most of the newer rods on the market have the line weight for which they are balanced marked somewhere on the shaft, reel seat, or butt. Match the numbers, and you can't go wrong. If the rod isn't marked, and the clerk at the sporting goods store doesn't know which weight to use, and you have followed my recommendations for an 8½ foot rod, go with a #7 or #8 line. Generally, either of those would be the proper weight for a rod of that length.

For terrestrial fishing, choose a floating line. Terrestrial insects are all either blown onto the water or jump there by accident, and the ones that do sink will sink far enough for effective fishing on the leader itself. Sinking lines are specialty items for fishing streamers and nymphs that are customarily fished on or near the bottom. They are harder to use, for both beginner and expert, since the line has to be picked up from under the water rather than from off the surface. The resultant drag, especially in long casts, is not only extremely fatiguing, but it can break the tip section of a rod if done improperly.

Fly lines come in three basic styles—level, double-taper, and weight-forward taper. Level lines are the cheapest, running between four and six dollars. Weight-forward tapers are among the easiest lines to cast, especially when using large, wind-resistant flies such as the hoppers, crickets, and cockroach. However, they do not permit really delicate presentation with the smaller flies. The double-taper is the best all-around line in my personal estimation, since all of the flies in this book may be cast effectively with it, and it has the added advantage of reversibility when one end becomes worn or is cut back to a point at which the taper is no longer effective in turning over the fly. Both weight-forward lines and double-tapers are expensive, ranging from thirteen to thirty dollars, but if they are kept clean and free from nicks and abrasions, they will last several seasons. I have one line—a double-taper—that was purchased twelve years ago and that is still as effective as it was the first day I put it on the rod. So, in effect, fly lines cost less in the long run than bait-casting or spinning lines, which must be replaced several times a season.

The floating lines of today are a far cry from the lines of the past, which had to be dressed constantly to keep them floating. They were made of silk, and had to be carefully and thoroughly dried at the end of each days's fishing in order to prevent rot.

Today's lines, however, are made of synthetics, and some of the latest lines are constructed of a core for strength surrounded by a layer of closed cell foam and covered by a very tough plastic for durability. These latest lines, albeit expensive, are virually unsinkable.

If your fishing will be limited to panfish and brackish water situations, with a few bass thrown in, an inexpensive level line will suffice, although it does not "turn over" as easily as the various tapers. I have used level lines in such situations for years—especially in brackish water, where the salt content and rock bottoms are hard on a line—

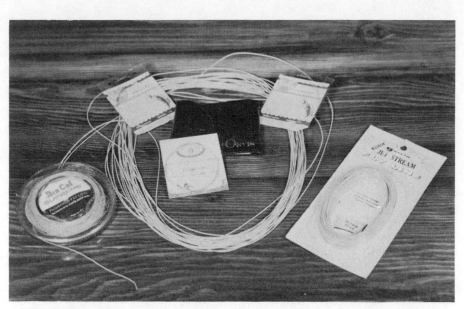

An Assortment of Fly Lines and Ready-Made Tapered Leaders

and doubt that I could have done better with tapered lines. The trouter, however, or the man concentrating solely on bass, may well appreciate the extra finesse and ease of casting that the tapered lines provide.

LEADERS

Leaders are the crucial connection between the fly and the line. They are made of monofilament, and many experienced fly-fishermen carry spools of different test lines (monofilament) in tests from ten to one-half pounds, making their own leaders as they need them. The advantage to this system is that when a tippet has been cut back, due to abrasion, wind knots, or just changing flies, a new tippet may be attached without scrapping the entire leader.

The process, however, is a lot of trouble, and since many of these hand-tied leaders consist of six or more lengths of different test monofilament, there are six or more knots in the leader—and each knot is a chance of failure, since the knot is the weakest point of any fishing rig.

By far the greatest boon that has come to fly-fishermen in many a year is the development of the knotless tapered leader. Several companies manufacture these leaders, at a cost of between twenty-five and fifty cents apiece—and they are well worth it both in time and trouble saved.

Admittedly, when the fine tips of these leaders are cut back, they are no longer effective for leader-shy trout. Nevertheless, they are inexpensive enough so that a goodly supply can be carried. Once they are cut back to a stiffer portion and the trout stop taking flies tied to them, wind them up and save them. Panfish, brackish water fish, and bass aren't nearly as particular. Let's face it—if a bass will take a plug or a plastic worm on twenty-pound test monofilament, he'll certainly hit a fly on a leader that tests four or five pounds.

In fact, the fly fisherman may, if he wishes, save even more money by using level leaders—straight lengths of transparent monofilament line—for bass and panfish. The only problem is that they don't turn over as easily as the tapered leaders, so there are times when the fly ends up in a bird's nest. While these snarls will occasionally put off bass, I have had bluegills and crappie nail the fly right out of the middle of the tangle.

Or, in the event that the trouter doesn't wish to burden himself with the racks of spools of different tests, one or two spools of light tippet material may be carried, and blood-knotted or nail-knotted to the cut-down tapered leaders when necessary. At least this only entails one extra knot in the rig, and is far more economical, both in time and money, than carrying eight or more spools of various test mono.

A word about leader length: many of the best trouters in the nation will tell you that nine-foot leaders are the absolute minimum, with twelve-foot being preferred. They are accurate—for shy trout in low water situations. For the beginner, these long leaders are difficult to cast, resulting in more snarls and wind knots than shorter lengths. While I always carry two or three nine-foot leaders with one-pound tippets, for fishing the tiny flies in low, clear water situations, my taste in leaders runs to the 7½-foot tapered leaders with tippets testing between two and six pounds—the lighter tippets used for panfish, the heavier employed for bass and brackish water fish. I have taken enough trout on 7½-foot leaders to make me certain that the loss of eighteen inches is not crucial, and the ease of casting more than makes up for the few trout I may have lost. I have also caught bass and panfish on trimmed back leaders that have ended up at four feet in length. The important point is to get the fly away from the heavy and highly visible fly line, laying the leader out straight with no bellies or loops to interfere with setting the hook.

CLOTHES

A fly-fisherman's clothes are dictated by the weather and the sort of fishing he does. A boat fisherman can wear almost anything that is comfortable for the season. The stream fisherman should have some sort of waders, either chest high or hip boots. Where the water is less than hip deep I much prefer the boots. They protect the legs from the water, are cooler in hot weather, can be rolled down below the knee for easier walking on dry land, are cheaper, permit access to trouser pockets, and can be more easily gotten out of if the fisherman steps in a deep hole.

In early season or relatively deep-water fishing, a pair of insulated, chest-high waders are a boon. They permit the daring angler to proceed through water almost to his armpits, keep him warm as well as dry, and in general give him access to more waters.

Some sort of hat should be worn, incidentally. The rays of the sun, which tan us so well on the beach when we are paying attention to it, can give severe burns and lead to skin cancer in unprotected fishermen who spend a lot of time on the water. A hat also provides some measure of protection when a gust of wind upsets the cast and the fly smacks into the back of your head. That is an embarrassing moment, certainly, but any fly-fisherman who tells you it has never happened to him is either lying or in for a nasty surprise at some time in the future. Nonetheless, it is better to be embarrassed on the stream than in a doctor's office, having the barb of a #2 hook cut out of your scalp.

A fly-fisherman's vest is a dandy little bit of clothing to have along. These vests are usually extremely light (until you load them up with all the things you want to carry) and the myriad pockets, rings, and straps make your tackle box a part of you. They are essentials for the stream fisherman, who cannot carry a box along, and many boat-bound fly-fishermen like them as well.

As a point of selection, I recommend that the novice fly-fisherman assemble all the gear that he wishes to carry before purchasing a vest. Then choose one with half again as many pockets, for the eventual addition of more boxes of flies. These vests come in a tremendous variety of styles and costs, and it is foolish to purchase one with more room than is really necessary. Any trip can be estimated as to the type of flies most likely to be needed, and at any rate, a full complement of terrestrials can be carried in as few as three large fly boxes. Add the other miscellaneous gear mentioned later in this chapter, and the vest is full.

But fly-fishermen, like all other fishermen, "collect" things. Rest assured that, if you purchase a vest with twenty pockets, you will fill those twenty pockets. And a vest that starts out weighing eight ounces can rapidly reach the eight-pound mark. Admittedly, eight pounds isn't an awful lot of weight—some bass fishermen's tackle boxes weigh over thirty pounds—but try wearing it and a pair of chest-high waders all day in midsummer!

Getting back to the subject of waders for a moment, you may find two different styles in the stores when you go to purchase them. There are those called "boot-foot waders" and there are those called "stocking-foot waders." The former have a "built in" shoe molded to the base of the wader; the latter are designed to be worn under wading shoes of either canvas or leather.

While all waders are subject to snags, tears, and holes, it has been my experience that the boot-foot waders are more durable and of heavier construction than the stocking-foot style. They, of course, are also hotter, but for the money spent they will give more trouble-free service than the other style.

FLY BOXES

Fly boxes are to the fly-fisherman what tackle boxes are to other fishermen. They contain the lures, and they come in a multitude of styles, from clear plastic boxes costing a few cents to sophisticated, compartmented works of art manufactured in England that cost more than many rods or reels. Nevertheless, a good fly box is very important, since it must provide easy access to the fly needed at the moment, be compact enough to carry easily, and protect the flies from crushing and becoming dulled.

For these reasons, on the stream I eliminate the clear plastic boxes from the list. They are fine for storing flies in bulk at home, since you can readily see what sorts of flies are in them when it comes time to replenish the stream boxes, even if they are stacked up. For these purposes, I prefer small boxes, or the newer, round, screw-together stack-packs, so that a single pattern and size may be kept in each box. It isn't necessary, certainly—compartmented plastic boxes will serve the same purpose—but it cuts a few minutes off a busy schedule for a few extra cents, and the boxes last indefinitely on the shelf.

They don't, however, last that long at streamside. The hinges on these boxes—no matter what the guarantees say—are not capable of holding up under the constant opening and closing that a fly-fisherman subjects them to. And a fly box with the hinges or the catch gone is worse than no fly box at all.

Speaking of no fly box at all, don't be taken in by the photos of serious-looking anglers carrying several dozen flies in their hat bands. A fleece hatband is all right for drying a fly or two in the open air before returning them to their boxes, but prolonged storage in the fleece will mat the feathers down and ruin their effectiveness. Occasionally, the minute flies will even get lost in the fleece. Rather than the hat band I prefer a little 2″ x 2″ square of fleece attached to the fishing vest pocket. It's handy there, and you don't forget that the flies are there.

The best boxes for the fisherman are the various seamless aluminum boxes that have brass hinges that don't rust, friction closures that don't snap off, and small compartments (sometimes with individual lids), coil springs, or aluminum clips inside to hold the flies individually. The two major manufacturers of these boxes are Wheatley of England and Perrine of the United States. By far, the Wheatley boxes are the most elite available, one model possessing clips in the lid and sixteen individually covered compartments for dry flies in the bottom—each

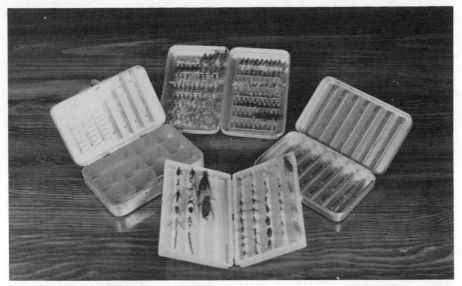

Fly Boxes

of the lids being individually hinged so that it can be opened in a high wind while leaving all of the other compartments sealed. At this writing, this box retails for thirty-three dollars, with a larger version, with thirty-two individually lidded compartments, selling for sixty dollars. These are boxes that you will pass on to your children, but they aren't necessary unless you want the finest tackle available at any price, and are prepared to pay for it.

For the average fly-fisherman, the Perrine boxes are a superb investment. They range between three and six dollars apiece, and come in a tremendous variety of styles. Their #92 dry-fly box and #96 wet-fly box, the former with coil springs, the latter with clips, are excellent for the terrestrial fisherman. Use the coil-spring box for flies with full hackle that shouldn't be matted down, the clip box for all others. In addition, they have a #95 box designed for salmon flies, with a swing-out leaf, which is one of the best boxes available for the large hoppers and crickets.

The midges and tiny ants pose a problem, since they won't fit under the clips in the wet-fly box, and the hooks are too fine for the coil springs to hold effectively. However, there are three alternatives available. Perrine puts out two boxes with compartments, and a single plastic cover for all of them at once. These are effective, although some of the smallest flies will "travel" between compartments, since the tolerances are not as close as they are in the Wheatley boxes. The second alternative is Perrine's #69 and #101 magnetic boxes, which have one entire side of the box lined in a magnetic material that holds the small flies effectively.

The third alternative is a box manufactured by Scientific Anglers, who also make balanced fly-casting systems. Their boxes possess full length plastic clips into which the bends of the hooks are pressed. Not only do they hold the small flies firmly but gently so as not to damage the hook, but, by holding the flies upright, they give complete protection to hackles. These boxes are relatively inexpensive—depending upon where they're purchased, they will run between two and three dollars, the latter price being straight retail cost. While they don't hold quite as many flies as the Perrine boxes, they are effective for all flies except the hoppers, crickets, and cockroach, and quite handy to use. The Scientific Anglers boxes are made of plastic with a built in, so-called lifetime hinge. I have owned two for several years and have never had any problems with the hinge, so I can recommend them as being virtually trouble-free, once you get the hang of putting the flies in and taking them out—those clips hold more firmly than you would imagine.

One word of warning: stay away from the Japanese imitations of the Perrine clip or coil-spring boxes. I have four of them that I will gladly give away. The clips are not only too wide, they are too loose to properly hold small flies, and the coil springs are wound so loosely that *no* flies will stay in place. In short, the money that you spend on them is wasted, because of the headaches that you will face because of them. Being of Scottish ancestry, I am for saving money wherever possible—but there are some cases in which a supposed savings is actually throwing money away.

NETS

If you intend to release all the fish that you catch, you'll be better off without a net. Simply reach down, following the leader with your fingers, grasp the fly and flip, and the fish will swim off without ever being touched—thus assuring that the mucus coating on its skin will not be damaged, thus promoting the growth of dangerous fungus. The fish will then have a better chance of survival.

However, there are times when you are going to want to keep a fish, either because you look forward to the taste of fish right out of the water, or because you have trapped a fish worth putting on a plaque. Because of the light tippet strength of most leaders, you cannot simply swing the fish into your hand.

There are two basic types of nets of use to the fly-fisherman: the stream net and the boat net, depending upon which type of fishing you are doing. The stream net is usually small (often called a trout net) with a short handle. Frames are made of either aluminum or wood, with the wood being better but considerably more expensive. Whichever frame you choose, make certain that the handle is attached to an elastic cord, which can be attached to a ring on your waders or vest. The elastic keeps the net out of the way when it isn't needed,

Stream-type Wooden Framed Net

but permits you to stretch out to net a fish that doesn't like the looks of your legs. Also insist upon a nylon net bag. Many of the cheaper nets have bags woven of cotton twine, which eventually rots and there is nothing more frustrating than fighting an eleven-pound brown trout for twenty minutes, only to have it fall through the bottom of the net, snapping the leader as it goes merrily on its way.

For the boat fisherman, who is usually in pursuit of bass or brackish water battlers, a different sort of net is in order. You haven't the maneuverability for netting in a boat that you have standing in a stream, so the net should have a relatively long handle, aluminum frame (wooden frames on these nets are simply too heavy to be practical), and, once again, nylon mesh.

If you fish with a fly rod, your net will be used quite frequently or very seldom, depending upon your reasons for fishing in the first place. Whatever use the net will receive, purchase a good one at the beginning. Those who take home a lot of fish will need it; those who only take home the lunkers will appreciate the fact that a good net won't go bad on them without their knowing it, failing at the crucial moment. Incidentally, on some of the less expensive nets the rubber hand grip will dry rot long before the nylon bag goes bad. Should this happen, simply purchase a bicycle hand grip and slip it over the aluminum handle. These grips are also effective on regular boat nets, giving a more comfortable and slip-free grip.

MISCELLANEOUS GEAR

There is simply no way of covering, in a book of this sort, all of the miscellaneous equipment that fly-fishermen may decide to carry with them. There are, however, a few articles that most anglers should have, or will eventually end up with. These brief descriptions will serve as a guideline for initial purchases. Receiving a few of the dream-book catalogs listed in the appendix will open up a whole world of things to tempt the angler—just make sure that what looks attractive is something that is really necessary, or you'll end up having to buy a donkey to carry your gear for you.

CLIPPERS: Leaders need to be trimmed, flies need to be cut off, and occasionally the inventive angler can "barber" a fly on the stream to more closely approximate the terrestrials that are on the water. Either a small pair of scissors or a toenail clipper may be used. I personally prefer the toenail clipper, since you won't get stabbed by it while bending over. There is an article on the market based on the toenail clipper, called an Angler's Pal, which contains not only the clipper, but a hook disgorger, knife blade, and bodkin (which is too large for practical use on most fly eyes). It is connected to a lanyard that is worn around the neck, so it is always handy. Since it costs little more than a straight pair of nail clippers, it may be a worthwhile investment for gadget-minded fishermen.

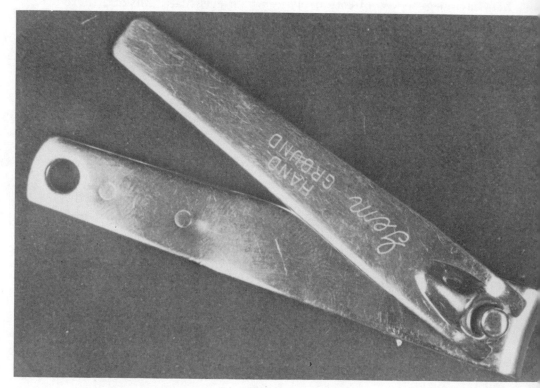

Clippers

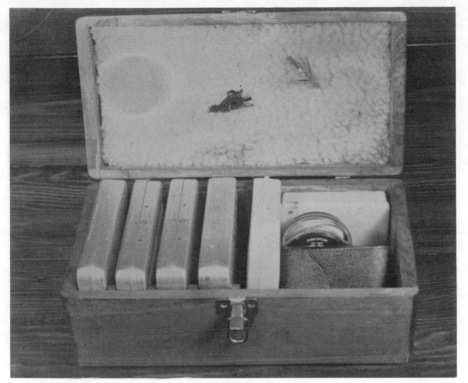

Tackle Box

MAGNIFYING GLASS: Just a small one will suffice. It is handy for examining hook points for dullness, and identifying small terrestrials found around the shore and on the water.

NEEDLE: A regular sewing needle can be kept in one of the fly boxes. It is handy for clearing head cement out of the eyes of flies. For easiest use, the eye end can be epoxied into the end of a short length of hardwood dowel. It gives you something more to grip, and less chance of running the eye into your finger.

TACKLE BOX: A tackle box, to contain fly boxes and other paraphernalia, is used by the boat fisherman rather than the streamside angler. Look for a spacious yet compact box, without cantelever trays (they aren't necessary), in which fly boxes may be stacked, with enough room for extra reel spools, the miscellaneous gear mentioned in this chapter, and perhaps a small streamside fly-tying kit. A box keeps all the gear together, and when you're ready to go all you have to do is grab the rod and the box.

CREEL: Creels are the standard means of keeping fish on the stream. The traditional creel is made of woven rattan, with a leather harness.

Creel and Stringer

There are also new collapsible canvas creels, which are quite inexpensive. The rattan creel, however, permits better air circulation, hence better cooling of the fish and less chance of spoilage.

STRINGER: For the boat fisherman, the stringer is the equivalent of the streamsider's creel. Stringers are actually better, since a fish in the water will live considerably longer than one in a basket. Do *not* simply use a string that goes through the gills. Such stringers kill the fish quickly, even in the water. The clip-style stringers on the market are inexpensive, last for years and years, and fish may even be released from them with little damage. Metal clip stringers are the cheapest, but occasionally a large fish, twisting against the stringer, can open the clips. The newer locking nylon stringers keep the fish alive and assure that they won't get away unless you release them.

15

TERRESTRIALS
FOR TROUT

If any of the readers have turned to these technique chapters expecting a full discourse on fly-fishing for the various species mentioned, they will be in for a disappointment. These chapters will assume a general knowledge of the habits of the various species, as well as a working knowledge of the fundamentals of fly casting; if these are not already a part of the reader's knowledge, a list of pertinent books will be found in the Bibliography, offering instruction in the art of fly casting, fly tying in general, and the habits and generalized techniques required for the various fish covered in the following chapters. The techniques covered here will apply only to the use of the terrestrial patterns mentioned in the preceding chapters.

We shall begin with trout, for the simple reason that when one mentions fly fishing in general the first picture that comes to mind is of a Theodore Gordon type on a clear stream, with a brace of trout laid out on the grassy sward beside the water. Fly fishing's beginnings were with the trout, so the association is a natural one.

However, until now trout fishermen have been more or less at the mercy of the mayfly hatches, with some reliance on caddis patterns, stoneflies, and a few others for the times when the mayflies weren't on the water. Matching those hatches has always been a pain in the neck for ninety percent of the trout fishermen, in spite of the fact that it has been the subject of innumerable books, most of which rehash the same information presented in the few classics on the subject.

To the terrestrial fisherman, hatches are unimportant, since even in the midst of a massive hatch of *Iron fraudator* a properly presented cricket, hopper, or beetle will take fish over and above a perfectly matched Quill Gordon. The reason for this effectiveness is quite simple;

Two-Pound Rainbow with Sowbug

in a perfectly matched hatch, the Quill Gordon will be one artificial among thousands of natural flies on the water, all looking pretty much alike. Therefore, the fish are more likely to take the naturals than the imitation simply because of the odds in the matter—one out of several thousand that the fraudulent *fraudator* will be selected.

But when, in the midst of all of these ¼″ flies, the selective trout spies an insect that it is used to feeding on at other times, an insect five or six times the size of the mayflies, the mere fact that the trout is feeding signifies that the larger flies will be more attractive to the hungry trout. Several writers have already noted this in the use of larger than normal flies of the imitator patterns—but the fallacy therein is that trout in general are very selective, and a 3/4" Quill Gordon *looks* artificial, whereas a 3/4" grasshopper *looks* natural. In effect, then, the trout fisherman who presents a large terrestrial to trout in the middle of a mayfly hatch may well be committing a heresy in tradition, but is in reality combining the best of two important theories —the larger-than-average fly with the exact imitation theory.

In addition, with more and more of our good trout waters disappearing, and the remaining ones becoming more and more difficult to reach, there has long been the need for a good searching fly to be used when the water is quiet and the trout are not in evidence. There have been a few works along the lines of the searching fly as well, some of which present interesting and sometimes effective solutions. However, reliance upon such insects as the caddis and the stonefly as searching patterns, no matter how effective they might be in the general run of fly fishing, is fallacious, due to the fact that there are many waters in which trout live that do not support either caddis *or* stoneflies; there are, however, no waters totally void of the appearance of terrestrial insects. Another factor to bear in mind is, once again, size. Trout that are not actively feeding, especially the older, larger trout that most of us covet, need real enticement to leave their lies for a single insect. Caddis and stone flies simply don't have the size necessary to draw these fish out on a regular basis. Hoppers, crickets, cockroaches, bees, and horseflies have the succulent appearance necessary to awaken the hunger pangs.

Of the nine species and subspecies of trout available to the fisherman, only three are pursued with enough general dedication to be worthy of coverage—the brown, the rainbow, and the brook trouts. The other species—lake trout, Dolly Varden trout, golden trout, Kamloops trout, cut-throat trout, and Piute trout—all have their own following, but their distribution is so limited as to retard the number of people who pursue them. For those fishermen who have access to these fish, the following information will be of value. The lake trout is seldom taken with flies of the wet or dry variety—usually streamers or spinners are employed—so this book has no real application to the pursuit of the lakers. However, the information given on the brook trout, in regard to both patterns and techniques, has proved effective when dealing with the Dolly Varden and the golden trout, and the same patterns and techniques applied to the rainbow have worked to good effect upon the Kamloops (which is often listed as a subspecies of the rainbow, anyway), the cut-throat trout, and the Piute.

The brown trout, *Salmo trutta,* is probably the most sought after of all the trouts in the United States, due in great part to the fact that it is the most widely distributed of the trouts, being able to live in much warmer water than the brook trout. It has also been transplanted to many waters throughout the country, and so is readily available to the greatest number of fishermen. An import from Europe, the brown trout was originally two separate species, the true brown and the Loch Leven trouts; with importation came cross- and interbreeding of the two species by fish culturists until the individual charactistics of both species had been blended together to create the fish that we today call the brown trout. Although the color of the fish varies considerably from location to location, there are certain distinguishing characteristics—notably, an enlarged adipose fin, scales that tend to be larger than those of the other trouts, and, no matter what the general overall color, there are almost always red spots on the sides of the brown trout, each spot surrounded by a light ring, ranging from almost white through light tan to yellow depending upon the locale from which the fish is taken.

The brown trout is attractive to the fisherman because of size as well. Many browns are taken between five and eight pounds, although $2\frac{1}{2}$ to three pounds is perhaps the average size. However, these do reach fifteen pounds or more in the United States, and a brown (Loch Leven) trout was taken in Scotland that tipped the scales at $39\frac{1}{2}$ pounds—a very good weight even for a lake trout.

The next most popular trout is the rainbow, which has been introduced in many of the same waters frequented by the brown. *Salmo gairdnerii*, however, has been introduced to the warmer waters of the south only more recently than the brown, and so is not yet as prevalent in the warmer waters as the brown. It is adapting well, however, and future years may see this fish prevalent in freshwater streams from San Diego and Georgia north.

The rainbow is a highly adaptable fish, and migrates from saltwater into freshwater rivers to spawn, although many of the fish spend their lives totally in fresh water. For this reason, coupled with the stocking programs, the rainbow is likely to spread rapidly, more rapidly than the brown, which is a territorial rather than a migratory fish.

The coloration of the rainbow gives the fish its name when living in fresh water; sea-run rainbows, often called steelheads, are a bright silver in color with a dark bluish or greenish back. The sea-run rainbows, or steelheads, are not as prone to the terrestrial patterns as are the rainbows of freshwater, although on the move from the sea to the sweetwater areas they will often take the larger terrestrial patterns, fished wet on a dead drift.

Rainbows are heavy for their length, with a $2\frac{1}{2}'$ fish weighing in the neighborhood of twelve pounds—another attractive feature for the fisherman. Most of the fish caught on the terrestrials average between two and ten pounds, although the larger fish are not as prone to take the smaller flies as are browns of the same size.

Rainbow Trout

Our final trout of general interest is the brook trout, *Salvelinus fontinalis*. This trout is the wild one, the most beautiful of all the trouts, at least in this author's opinion. The brook trout is not as widely distributed as are the brown and the rainbow, for it requires cold, clear water, and cannot tolerate the warmth that the other trouts can. The brook trout is not a native west of the Mississippi, but it has been transplanted there in mountain streams and lakes, and is doing well. In some areas of the more northern climates the brookie goes to sea, but over most of its range it stays in fresh water. The brook trout is the terrestrial man's dream, since most of the areas in which it is found are overrun by various terrestrial insects—many of which make the fisherman's trip hell on earth with their bites and stings, but which also provide a fish that is used to feeding on terrestrial patterns eighty percent of the time.

The scales of the brook trout are exceptionally small, and the color, while ranging from light to very dark, is beautifully mottled. The lower fins are red, while all the fins have bright white edges. The record brook trout weighed over fourteen pounds, but the angler today will be lucky to find one over eight. On the average brookies run between two and four pounds, with the greatest number on the smaller side. Nevertheless, the brookie is a beautiful fish, and well worth the work it takes to get him—work that will be greatly lessened through the use of terrestrial patterns.

There is no point in dealing with specialized techniques for the various species of trouts. It makes interesting reading, but it simply isn't true. The factor that determines the techniques that must be employed is the type of water you are fishing, not the fish you are after.

What is important, however, is the pattern used. Before we cover water types and the techniques required for fishing each variety, the following charts will provide the fly-fisherman with the proper patterns to be used for each species. Where there are different preferences between Eastern and Western fish, separate lists have been provided.

Brown Trout

Eastern	Western
Letort Hopper	Quill Bodied Hopper
Deer Hair Hopper	Deer Hair Hopper
Muddler Minnow	Dave's Hopper
Letort Cricket	Muddler Minnow
Deer Hair Cricket	Deer Hair Cricket
Yellow Woolly Worm	Brown Woolly Worm
Hammer Fly	Black Woolly Worm
Deerfly	Brown Beetle
Greenbottle Fly	Black Beetle
Green Deer Hair Worm	Red Ant
Red Ant	Cinnamon Ant
Black Ant	Green Deer Hair Worm
Black Beetle	Deerfly
Japanese Beetle	Horsefly
Sowbug	

Letort Hopper	Dave's Hopper
Deer Hair Hopper	Muddler Minnow
Red Ant	Black Ant
Black Ant	Red Ant
Velvet Ant (Southern range)	Cinnamon Ant
Black Beetle	Black Beetle
Brown Beetle	Brown Beetle
Japanese Beetle	Green Deer Hair Worm
June Bug	Deerfly
Inchworm	Horsefly

Two-and-a-Half-Pound Rainbow Shown with Rod and Box of Terrestrials

Hammer Fly
Deerfly
Thrip
Sowbug
Cress Bug
Cockroach (Sea-run)

Sowbug
Cress Bug

Brook Trout

Letort Hopper
Letort Cricket
Brown Woolly Worm
Yellow Woolly Worm
Hammer Fly
Deerfly
Housefly
Greenbottle Fly
Green Deer Hair Worm
Inchworm
Red Ant
Black Ant
Cinnamon Ant
Deer Hair Leafhopper
Potato Leafhopper
Rose Leafhopper
Lateral Leafhopper
Black Beetle
Brown Beetle
Japanese Beetle
June Bug
Thrips
Sowbugs
Cress Bugs

The brook trout in the West behaves in the same manner as its Eastern counterparts. Use the Eastern patterns. The brookie feeds most regularly on smaller insects, unlike the Western counterparts of the other two species.

Armed with the proper patterns and the proper tackle for the fish, every other key to success depends upon using the proper technique for the type of water in which the fish are found. Once the techniques have been mastered, and the patterns selected, any failure to catch fish will simply mean that there are no fish to be caught.

For the lake fisherman, after browns, rainbows, or brookies, technique is rather simple, since lakes present only one type of water. In lake fishing for trout, the key to using the terrestrials is to look for overhangs. These overhangs may take the form of trees fallen in the water, trees that merely extend over the water (no matter what height above the surface), undercut banks, and shorelines with tule and other grasses bending over the water's surface.

Fishing lakes from the shore itself is very awkward, since the fly must, in most cases, land within only a few inches of the shore itself.

The two exceptions are the landflies and the bees, which can land on the water at almost any location. However, because of the sporadic nature of their falling into lakes, the fish tend to congregate in the sheltered areas under the overhangs, awaiting the insects that fall from those overhangs into the water directly above them.

In fishing the lakes, therefore, fly casting from a boat and wading are the two most productive methods. Boat fishing permits the fly caster to drive the fly directly under overhanging branches, which is perhaps the most deadly of the techniques; but unless the caster has managed to learn his casting technique while sitting, he presents a much higher silhouette while standing in the boat, and thus has a greater chance of being noticed by the fish.

Most fly-fishermen, therefore, would choose to wade the shorelines; and for this style of fishing I highly recommend the perfection of the side cast and roll cast in addition to the standard overhead cast. With the side cast, the wading fisherman can present the fly under overhanging branches as effectively as can the boat fisherman, and with the mastery of the roll cast, which keeps the line and the fly low to the water, he can present the lure into hidden pockets that not even the boat fisherman can reach, including actually putting the fly under undercut banks, into the dark hollows where the largest fish often lie.

Woolly Worms in all patterns, the green deer hair worm, the inchworm, the leafhoppers, and the ants are the most effective patterns

Pool with Overhangs

for fishing under overhanging trees, since these are the types of insects most likely to fall out of the trees. For undercut banks, the preference runs to sowbugs, beetles, and crickets—the grounddwellers; and for fishing the overhanging grasses, the best patterns are the grasshoppers as the top number, followed by leafhoppers, ants, and inchworms, in that order.

For trees and undercut banks, the best method is to simply sidecast or rollcast the fly onto the water's surface in the normal manner. However, a deadly technique where overhanging grass is present is to cast the fly onto the overhanging grass itself, twitch it lightly, and then drop it off the grass into the water. This method is especially effective if the grass itself touches the water, since the twitching action will disturb the water's surface and draw the attention of the fish. I personally have had some explosive strikes the instant the fly hit the water by using this method, and in a few cases have had the trout come out of the water to meet the fly in midair. Apparently the fish are so used to feeding from the grasses that they watch the waving tips for any movement that would signify an insect about to fall into the water above them.

By far, however, the greatest amount of trout fishing is done in streams, and streams present several different types of water along their length, each of which requires a different technique. The basic types of water encountered along streams are riffles, pools, bends, and, as in the case of lake fishing, overhangs. In addition, there are two basic types of stream—the woodland, or forest, stream, and the meadow stream. Different techniques and patterns are required on these divergent varieties of streams as well.

Without doubt, meadow streams are the easiest to fish. There is room for the overhead cast, which is the only cast that many novice fly-fishermen have mastered; meadow streams can be fished from the shore, since they are generally narrow enough so that the angler standing on one shore can present the fly to the opposite shore; the meadow grasses usually provide a modicum of concealment; and the water types within the particular stream can be read from a distance, allowing the angler to prepare his assault in advance.

Forest streams, however, are much more difficult to fish. Overhanging trees and brush, while providing much falling food for the fish, hinder casting tremendously; in most cases, fishing from shore means standing right at the water's edge, and flicking the fly such a short distance that often only the leader passes the rod tip; the proximity of trees to the shore and the necessity of the fly-fisherman being on the water eliminates much of the concealment that meadow grasses offer; and the bends, log falls, and tree growth in and around forest streams make it difficult if not impossible to read the water in advance.

Nevertheless, more good trout, that is, large, wild trout, are caught in forest streams than in meadow streams. The angler willing to take

Stream Emerging from Forest into Meadow

the extra trouble to fish the woodland streams has a greater chance of finding fish, for the simple reason that few people will actually take that trouble, and therefore the woodland streams have less fishing pressure.

Patterns for the meadow streams include all the grasshopper patterns, the crickets, ants, leafhoppers, and the green deer hair worm and inchworm. The forest stream lends itself to crickets, ants, woolly worms, beetles, landflies, thrips, sowbugs, and cockroaches. And while the meadow stream can be fished with long, delicate overhead casts, the forest stream technique involves short casts, roll casts, and sometimes merely stripping line and letting the current carry the fly downstream from the angler's standing position.

It goes without saying that the angler of the forest stream must wade. There is no other effective way of working the water. And while the meadow stream fisherman has the added advantage of being able to work upstream, the forest man must follow the current, since he hasn't the room to present a long enough cast upstream to be effective. The chief drawing factor to all of the extra work involved on the forest stream is that the fish present in these waters generally average 1½ to two pounds heavier than their meadow dwelling counterparts.

The water types found in streams—that is, riffles, pools, and bends—are the same in both meadow and forest streams, so there is no need to differentiate between the stream types in a discussion of these varieties of water. Riffles occur when the water flows at a rather vigorous pace

Logfalls cause pools when water is trapped behind them.

148

over a shallow area in the stream, generally a sand or gravel bar. Because of the shallow nature of the water, riffles are almost always clear, and any fish in them can spot the angler readily. They can also spot incompetent presentations of the flies, so the utmost care must be taken; however, riffles are worth the trouble, since the fast water carries insect life to the mouths of the waiting fish.

Trout are usually found at the tails of riffles, where the water starts deepening again, facing into the current. They will lie quite still in these locations, finning only enough to stabilize themselves in the water, since the action of the current itself not only brings them food, but also carries oxygen through their gills, eliminating the need for motion to obtain that circulation. These trout watch the water carefully, because food moving with the current can easily be swept by them. When they strike, they strike quickly and savagely.

The shallow water of the riffles requires a fine tippet—5X to 7X — of nine to twelve feet in length. Coarser or shorter tippets can be seen by the trout in water such as this, and will prevent them from striking. Due to the fineness of the tippets and the clarity of the water, only the smaller fly patterns should be used—Letort Crickets in the smallest sizes, ants, thrips, leafhoppers, and the landflies. Ants and leafhoppers are especially effective. Beetles can be used in forest streams, but only in the smaller sizes.

The riffle is the place for the dead drift, and so can be used with the same effect in both meadow and forest stream. The fly is presented at the head of the riffle, where the water turns fast, and enough line played out on the water to permit the fly to drift approximately four feet past the tail of the riffle. If a fish has not struck by that time, chances are slim of him picking it up any farther along.

It is imperative in fishing the riffles with terrestrials that no drag whatsoever be imparted to the fly. It must float rapidly and freely, to simulate an insect that has fallen into the fast water and is being carried along. Very few insects struggle in fast water, so there can be no movement to the fly other than that imparted by the current itself.

If it is possible to fish a given riffle from the shore, approach the center of the riffle, but stay well concealed. Present the fly at the head of the riffle, let it float past the tail, and, if there is no strike, pick up the line and cast again; generally six or eight casts will show if a trout is in residence. If, in the case of woodland streams, the fly must be floated straight down from the head of the riffle itself, allow at least fifteen minutes to pass before casting after you have picked up the line, since the line pick-up will be evident to any trout present. This is time-consuming, but very large trout are frequently taken from riffles, so, if there is any evidence of trout in the stream, the wait could be well worthwhile.

Other areas in riffles where fish are likely to be found are the downstream sides of rocks or logs that may have lodged themselves on

Bend in stream with overhanging ferns is perfect trout lie.

the bar that forms the riffle. These obstructions cause eddies, which swirl the water around, as well as a calm spot directly downstream of the obstruction. Dead drifts moving closely past these obstructions frequently find trout—the angler should make at least one drift past each side of the rock or log, to make certain that the fly passes the direction in which the trout is facing.

Bends in the stream are fished in somewhat the same way as riffles,

150

and for pretty much the same reasons. Whenever a flowing stream makes a bend, the flow of the water is speeded up, and eddies are created in the elbows of the bends. If the water is moving fast enough, there may even be miniature whirlpools that create a vortex to trap small insects. Trout will lie right against the bank, or under overhanging shoreline, at these bends, waiting for the current to bring insects into their lies.

In situations such as this, any of the terrestrial patterns may be used, depending upon the species of trout you are after (see pattern charts). Bends are easier to fish than riffles, especially in the forest streams, since, when the fly is finally carried out of the bend by the current, the water will also carry the line away from the trout's lie, and the line and fly may then be picked up off the water without unduly disturbing the fish. For this reason the bends can be covered more thoroughly than the riffles, with subsequent casts and pattern changes.

Larger patterns can be used here than in the riffles, since the water in the bends has usually cut deeply into the earth and the water, although moving rapidly, does not lend itself as readily to the fish's perception of leader and line. Tippets here can go as high as 1X or even OX, and heavier tippets are often needed in the case of large browns.

Overhangs all along the streams, both meadow and forest, should be fished in the same manner as lake overhangs, putting the fly as far into the pockets as is possible. In many cases on the streams, fishing the overhangs must be done by feel alone, even if using dry fly terrestrials, since the fly will be lost to view. Keep a tight line, and at the slightest divergence from normal drift, strike.

The final water variety of importance to the terrestrial fisherman after trout is the pool, and the pool is perhaps the most important of all. The pool in the stream can be formed in many ways—by a natural slowing and widening of the stream for a distance; by a tree against which the water has backed up after it has fallen into the water; by backing up against beaver dams; and through many other natural and artificial occurrences. It is calm water, often clear, but sometimes stained dark by leaf mold. The leaf mold also frequently lends a soft bottom to the pool, and the ground around it is rich from the constant moisture and decaying leaves. These pools are found mostly in the forest streams, and contain a wealth of fish due to the wealth of insect life in the area.

In the pools, the most effective patterns are woolly worms, grasshoppers, crickets, ants, beetles, sowbugs, and cockroaches, with the larger patterns often outfishing the smaller ones by a wide margin.

The technique in working the pools is to keep the casts short and cover the surface of the water thoroughly, since fish in the pools can be just as easily found in the middle as against the shorelines. Also,

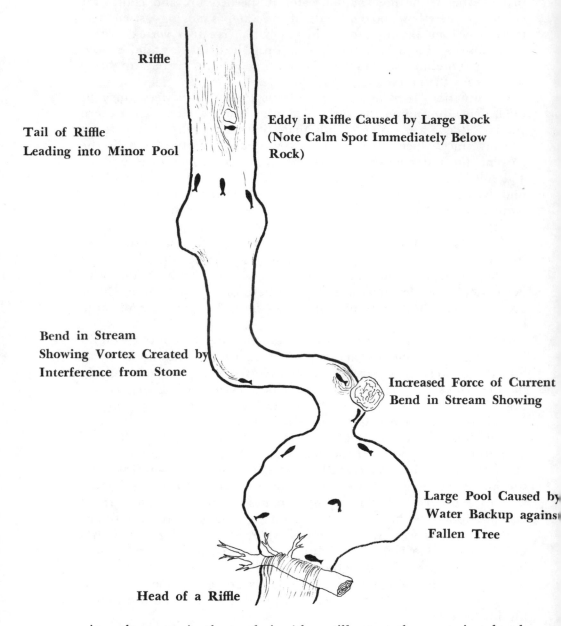

Riffle

**Tail of Riffle
Leading into Minor Pool**

**Eddy in Riffle Caused by Large Rock
(Note Calm Spot Immediately Below
Rock)**

**Bend in Stream
Showing Vortex Created by
Interference from Stone**

**Increased Force of Current
Bend in Stream Showing**

**Large Pool Caused by
Water Backup against
Fallen Tree**

Head of a Riffle

since the water in the pools is either still or, at the most, just barely moving, some action must be imparted to the flies.

The most effective method of doing this is to allow the fly to drop and remain still for ten or fifteen seconds. Then lightly twitch the rod tip, or tap the butt of the rod lightly with the palm of your hand, causing the fly to twitch slightly on the water. Wait until all the ripples

Typical Forest Stream Seen from Head of Riffle

have faded, and repeat. The result gives the appearance of an insect that has accidentally fallen into the surface film and is struggling to get to shore. It can be deadly.

By and large, fish the grasshoppers in the middle of the pool, and the others closer to shore, since the hoppers are the only ones really likely to end up in the middle, unless trees overhang the full width of the pool. In that case, any pattern for use in the pool can be fished in the center. Some of the largest brook trout caught today are taken from pools just such as those.

Try the terrestrials on trout your next time out. You may well find yourself dropping your mayfly patterns into Clorox to bleach off the materials. After all, the hooks used for mayflies are just perfect for ants, thrips, landflies, and leafhoppers.

16

TERRESTRIALS FOR BASS

The black bass is the freshwater big game for the terrestrial fisherman. While it is extremely doubtful that the next world's record bass will be taken on the fly rod, fish of up to ten pounds are not rare, and any time an angler can tangle with a ten-pound chunk of solid fighting fury in a weed- and snag-infested body of water and bring the fish to the net with the fly rod, he has accomplished more than the salmon fisherman who lets the current tire his fish before tailing it.

There are three major species of black bass in the United States— the largemouth, *Micropterus salmoides*; the smallmouth, *Micropterus dolomieu*; and the spotted, or Kentucky bass, *Micropterus punctulatus*. All three will take the terrestrials, the smallmouth a bit less often, the chief reason being that smallmouth are most often found deep in clearwater lakes or in swift-flowing, gravel-bottomed streams. In the former location they will not readily rise to take insects, preferring to feed upon fishes instead; in the latter, a fly is so often swept over their heads too rapidly to be noticed that such topwater fishing is unreliable at best. There are, however, situations in which the smallmouth may be taken, and these will be covered later in this chapter.

The largemouth is the favorite of the terrestrial fishermen, simply because he is so extremely cooperative. He is found in almost every type of water, from slow-moving forest streams to large rivers, and from quarter-acre farm ponds to huge, natural lakes and man-made impoundments. He ranges from coast to coast, and from Florida to Canada; in fact, there are few places in the country that are not within an hour's drive of excellent largemouth fishing .

In addition to his range, the largemouth lives up to his monicker. The fish is a voracious eater, consuming anything within range that

155

Casting from a reedy shore can produce many cruising bass.

he can get into his mouth—and that includes snakes, ducklings, and baby muskrats as well as all varieties of insect life. He prefers slow or calm waters, which makes him the ideal target for the terrestrial angler, who can manipulate an imitation in the calm surface tension to simulate the struggles of a dying insect—a move that drives the largemouth right out of the water in a crash and flurry.

Bass fishing is not the realm for small flies and light tippets. Many of the fish taken will come from the middle of the thickest jungles of vegetation imaginable, and there is no time for finesse until the fish has been removed from this jeopardy into open water where it can be played safely. Either tapered or level leaders may be used, but for largemouths they should not test lighter than six pounds—go heavier if you are comfortable with the stiffer monofilament, because snags and snapped tippets are commonplace.

Fly-fishing for bass is certainly not new; as soon as anglers discovered, probably by accident, that the bass would take a fly, a whole new realm of fly-fishing opportunity was opened for those without access to trout waters. But bass fishing with the long rod has come a long way since its institution.

The first rods for bass were typically salmon rods, with many anglers believing the tremendous length and stiffness of the whitewater rods necessary for taking bass consistently. In part they were right—at the time. The salmon-type fly rods were quite heavy and tiring to use, but until the development of the newer tapered lines and some changes in fly construction and patterns, they were necessary to fling the monstrous creations used to tempt bass.

Bass flies for too long a period of time were simply greatly enlarged versions of trout flies—especially of bright patterns like the Parmachene Belle and Yellow Sally. These were attractor patterns, and almost always fished wet.

Then someone came along and started tying large, bushy dry flies for largemouths, and the thrill of topwater, smashing strikes—a thrill unmatched in *any* form of trout fishing—was realized. These large dries, such as the Sofa Pillow, were effective enough, but they eventually soaked up so much water that casting them became akin to having a soggy bird tied to the end of the tippet.

So, the Deer Hair Bug was born. At last there was a high floating, large, lightweight fly that, when it started to become waterlogged, could be squeezed partially dry and would continue to float. Yet, still a problem presented itself: the very bulk of the fly, coupled with its light weight, brought wind resistance into the casting picture, and in gusty winds the bugs could not be cast with any accuracy. Then came the cork bodied poppers and their relatives, slightly overcoming the problem of wind resistance by giving greater density for the size of the "fly," but once again increasing the weight that had to be cast.

Finally, only the wind-resistant Deer Hair Bugs were even vaguely

This seven-pounder fell victim to a large hopper imitation snaked under an overhanging tree.

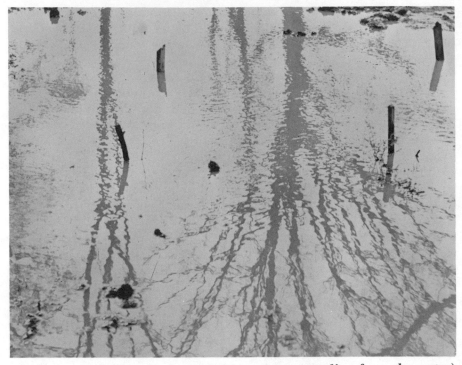

Stickups (submerged stumps and branches protruding from the water) are an ideal target for the terrestrial fisherman.

imitative, and a search of various fly-fishing catalogs will turn up very few imitative patterns even today.

Now, it stands to reason that any fish, no matter how voracious it may be, is going to prefer feeding upon those creatures that it is used to taking in any given season. Few anglers have had the thrill of seeing a school of largemouths literally churning the water to a froth, and even fewer have been able to say after such an experience that they had caught and released so many that their arms became tired from fighting fish rather than from false casting. And yet, in late summer, when largemouths (according to some experts) are supposed to be sulking in thirty feet of water, I have stood on a grassy shore at dawn, just as the sun was beginning to warm the grass, and fought schooling bass that were boiling the water as they attacked morning-lethargic grasshoppers that were being blown onto the surface of a farm pond.

There is a very important point to bear in mind when fishing for largemouth bass and trying to correlate actual experience with the writing of many of the "bass pros." When these men speak of deep-water structure and bass being suspended thirty feet below the surface in August, many fly fishermen hang up their rods until fall. Bass simply will not rise thirty feet to take a surface fly. That much is certainly true.

158

But what many of us fail to realize is one of the most obvious points of any sort of fishing—so obvious that it may sound ridiculous to even mention, yet that all too many fly-fishermen forget in the welter of bassing information that comes their way. In order for fish to be in thirty feet of water, there has to *be* thirty feet of water! There is simply no way on earth that a bass can be in thirty feet of water if he lives in a farm pond that is five feet deep.

So, while the bass pros are charging around thousand-acre reservoirs with their fish finders, spoons, jigs, and deep-plunging plugs, trying to find concentrations of bass and picking up a few now and then, there is a vast number of "bass amateurs" waggling around the shores of two- or three-acre ponds, using their eyes to look for pad beds (and seeing a wealth of other things in the process) and catching bass consistently. Admittedly, these may not be ten-or twelve-pounders; there are precious few of those which fall to *anyone's* lure, but they are the ones you always hear about. But there will be lots of fish in the one- to three-pound category, and occasionally bass up to seven and eight pounds that may be tempted with a hopper, cricket, or other fly. And personally, I would rather fight a two-pounder in the shallows on a five-pound tippet than dredge a three-pounder from thirty feet of water with thirty-pound test line and a lure that weighs almost as much as the fish—and puts up more water resistance.

The key to bass fishing with the terrestrials is a word that has become common vocabulary with bass fishermen of all sorts: *structure.* Now, the term *structure,* as well as other terms in the basser's vocabulary, is relatively new only in the sense of the word itself. When I was in my salad days we fished the same sort of water, looking for the same things, only we had, let us say, a thinner dictionary. Dad never said "Work the structure" or "Hit the stickups" or "The locater says there's a submerged road with three major ruts right under the boat." If I remember correctly, he said "Look, son [or Dummy, depending upon where the fly hit] you won't catch bass in wide open water; put the fly [expletives deleted] next to that stump."

If you are one of the modern bassers, add whatever words you want to your sport. At least then you'll be able to talk to the pros (if they'll talk to you) on their own level—but you won't catch any more bass. Keep it simple; as the old man once told me, the simpler you keep your language, the better off you are: for example, never ask your wife to buy a fifth of scotch—just tell her to get you a bottle. Most of the time you'll end up with a quart.

The same is true with bassing. The word structure is all encompassing, and the so-called pros use it to identify everything from a tree fallen in the water to a five-foot diameter, one-foot-deep depression in the middle of a five-thousand-acre reservoir. For the fly-fisherman—the terrestrial fisherman looking for action with a brawling fish—structure means anything in shallow water that provides a place for bass to hide. It might be a fallen tree, or a flooded forest of stumps (either above or just below the surface) or a grass bed, or an expanse of lily pads. It might even be a boat dock or an old duck blind.

The important thing is that there is something in the water that is different from the surrounding water, and for the terrestrial fisherman, you don't need any fancy equipment to locate it. Forget sunken horse trails and minidepressions in deep water; the fish won't rise. Simply look for a change in the shoreline, and drop the fly in or near that change—the closer the better.

And don't be fooled by the depth of the water, either. I have pulled bass that topped seven pounds out of water only a foot deep. If a bass has shade—its most important requisite—it will be found in water just deep enough to cover its back. Many times, in shadows with so little water that a person wouldn't think a bass could get wet, I have seen the fish charge the flies with their backs out of the water.

An important point to bear in mind is that bass will not sip the lure as trout will. The strike of a bass is often violent, always forceful. Be prepared to set the hook immediately, and with force, since a bass has a much tougher mouth than a trout. Be prepared as well to horse the bass for a few yards, to get it out of the thick of things, if you don't want to lose it. I have yet to meet a bass that wasn't a better knot-tier than I am when it comes to wrapping a leader around submerged limbs or lily pad stems.

The patterns that have given the best success on largemouth bass are as follows:

> All the grasshopper imitations, in sizes 8 on up.
> Deer Hair Cricket
> Woolly Worms (all patterns)
> Green Deer Hair Worm
> Horsefly
> Bumblebee
> Wasp
> Honeybee
> Cockroach
> Black Beetle
> Japanese Beetle
> Sowbug
> Deerfly
> Greenbottle Fly

As you can see, these are all patterns with some size to them. Large-mouths won't take the smaller patterns, even if you play them over the fish's head for an hour. I have seen small largemouths take leafhoppers, but only when hundreds of them were blown onto the water, and then the fish would suck in many at a time. Another factor is that, in most of the places where bass are found, there will also be bluegills and

In heavily structured bass water, a large pattern affixed to the end of a light spinning rig with a bobber six feet from the fly will mean more bass brought to shore.

other species of panfish. These smaller fish will give you enough trouble by hitting even the largest offering (Roy Weil, a superb stream fisherman with a plug, has often taken six-inch bluegills on five-inch Rapala minnow plugs while plugging for bass), but they will eliminate all chances of having a bass meet the steel if the flies are small.

The trick to taking bass on terrestrials isn't really much of a trick at all. Trout are often more selective than bass, but after years of study I have come to the conclusion that a bass is the smartest freshwater fish. It knows what regularly falls on the water, and where it falls. If a trout is used to eating sowbugs, it will take them even in the middle of a lake. Bass on the prowl will take hoppers in the middle, but my experience has shown that they will only take sowbugs near undercut banks, where the living insect will be more likely to fall. There will undoubtedly be those anglers out there who will read this book and will take a ten-pounder on a sowbug in the middle of Santee-Cooper reservoir and will write to tell me how wrong I am. Well, part of the fun of fishing is the fact that some things happen out of the norm—I will be the first to admit that. Nevertheless, for the beginner, it is best to read the water and the shoreline at the same time, and offer the species of insects that are most likely to end up struggling in the surface tension.

The most profitable location for bass fishing with the terrestrials is, as in the case of lake fishing for trout, under overhanging structure. Largemouths like to lie under eroded banks and beneath drooping trees, not only because of the protection they afford, but also because of the amount of food that this sort of structure provides for them. The fly should be cast as close to the structure as possible—remember that bigger fish won't move far for their meals—and this also means that the fly must often be put into the thickest part of a tangle if the fish is to strike.

The type of shoreline terrain will determine the fly to use unless there are actually insects on the water. In farm ponds and many lakes where the shore is part of a field that slopes gently to the water, with long, overhanging grasses or grain crops, the primary choices are Woolly Worms in spring, Wasps and Bees in early to midsummer, and Grasshoppers in late summer to early autumn. These flies should be cast to land anywhere from the very verges of the shore to ten feet out, depending upon the length of the structure and the prevailing winds, as well as the depth of the water. Obviously, if the water in a lake suddenly drops to twenty feet deep at a point five feet from shore, a cast that lands ten feet from shore will *not* take bass. However, if the water is shallow—less than six feet—and stumps and other structures are present for a great distance from shore, then casts that fall closer to the boat may well take the fish. Each piece of water must be read individually, and the placement of the fly determined by the depth of water as well as the other factors already mentioned.

Incidentally, don't be worried about long casts in order to avoid spooking the fish. Carl Bracken, one of the best men with a fly rod nowadays, believes that a close approach to a fish is not necessarily going to spook it. His theory is that short, light, accurate casts are far more important than shadows on the water, as long as the approach is made quietly. As a man who was raised in the old style of casting as

The best sort of largemouth waters.

far as you could so the fish wouldn't know there was anyone around, I was justifiably skeptical of his approach—until I saw him take bass less than ten feet from the boat as he eased his way through structure.

There is a great deal of validity behind Carl's reasoning, and a fisherman only has to take a trip under water to find out. The belief that a bass can see you coming is only partly true; it can see the boat, because the boat extends under water. So do your legs if you are wading. But in regard to seeing the man standing in a boat above water, the case becomes more vague. With both the refractive and reflective qualities of water, all a bass can possibly see is a shadowy outline—and that only if the water is perfectly calm. If there is the slightest breeze to ruffle the water, that shadowy outline is broken up even more, to the point that the bass cannot determine whether or not the outline is that of a man or a tree. The next time you are swimming, have someone stand in the water near you, and, from beneath the water, look toward them. Their legs will be clearly defined, but their upper bodies will be little more than a haze. In stump-infested water, bass will not be able to determine your presence. I have taken enough bass on short casts to prove it at least to my own satisfaction.

Now, back to structure and shorelines. Grassy verges are only a part of the shorelines faced by bass fishermen: in many cases, forest will

A four-pounder that took a deerfly in water only nine inches deep.

grow directly to the water's edge. In that case, the patterns will be Woolly Worms and the Green Deer Hair Worm in the spring, landfly and beetle imitations in early to midsummer, and flies, bees, wasps, cockroaches, and sowbugs in late summer to early autumn. In late autumn the bass go on a feeding spree in order to prepare for the lean times of winter, and any of the large terrestrials will be effective (to be perfectly honest, late autumn is not a fair test of any fly pattern— or any other lure, for that matter—since I have seen bass in October strike cigarette filters that someone had thrown into the water) .

Stream largemouths—and when I say stream, I mean the headwaters of major rivers as well—are gauged once again by the type of terrain through which the water flows. However, many river headwaters flow through forests rather than fields, and the novice, in reading the water, would be tempted to eliminate hopper imitations from his repertoire.

The point to bear in mind is that the water in these areas is flowing, and hence carrying food from areas above it. Stream largemouths are generally well fed, and so to be tempted they must be presented with large flies. In spite of the recommendations for lake fishing, I would not even attempt fishing a stream without hopper imitations. These, beetles, cockroaches, crickets, sowbugs, landflies, and yellow jackets are the most effective flies for this sort of fishing, and in that order.

Riffles in this sort of water, while looking ideal for trout, are not the places to cast for bass. Again, the key word is *structure,* and you have to differentiate bass structure from trout structure to a certain extent. Look for bass only in the places that you would look for lunker trout—deep holes, undercut banks, stillwater places next to fallen trees, and eddies behind rocks. Check the current and, if at all possible, try to get the fly to drift into these locations. Generally these places are small, and even a short, light cast with a large fly might spook the fish.

Stream and river bass will come farther for the fly than will lake or pond bass. They are used to catching their food on the move as the current carries it downstream, and strikes are likely to be fast and violent, with little or no warning. Most streams and river headwaters that harbor bass don't provide much room for playing with the fish— there are simply too many things that can go wrong. However, the fast action, the smashing strikes, and the aerial acrobatics of the bass in these shallow waters more than make up for the number of fish that will throw the hook or snap the line on a submerged tree.

While the moving water of a stream often permits a simple drift, as in the case of trout fishing, lake fishing and the stillwater eddies of some river fishing call for movement of the fly. Cockroaches, beetles, and sowbugs can struggle their way across the surface for a good distance, so these flies are good for steady retrieves by twitching in shallow waters. Grasshoppers, crickets, and landflies are rather helpless when they hit the water, in spite of their struggles, so these patterns should be allowed to drift naturally in streams and twitched only slightly and periodically in lakes and river eddies. One very effective means of creating the struggling appearance is to keep a tight line and strike the rod butt with the heel of your hand. The resultant vibrations that run down the line create the proper minor twitchings of a half-drowned insect fighting for its life.

Kentucky or spotted bass can be fished for following the same methods as used for the largemouth, but smallmouth bass are a different story. Where they are found in relatively shallow streams and rivers, the hopper imitations (especially the Muddler Minnow) and the beetles take the most fish. Smallmouth fishing in lakes, with the exception of early spring when the bass are on the nests (and not always then) is more within the realm of the live bait, spinner, spoon, and plug fisherman than the fly-fisherman, since the fish are generally too deep for a topwater fly to be effective. In stream fishing for smallmouths, work riffles that lead to calm water, trying to drift the flies so that they swing by large rocks that break the flow of the water. Strikes will come fast and hard, but they are fewer and farther between than when fishing for largemouths.

There is much discussion of which is a better fighter, the largemouth or the smallmouth. The general consensus seems to be that the smallmouth is a stronger battler, and I used to be upset about the fact that I preferred the largemouth. But then I thought about the type of water in which each was found, and I remembered a very apt comment made by Jason Lucas, one-time fishing editor of *Sports Afield*: "Even a leaky boot puts up a good fight in a fast current." Take the largemouth on a fly rod in a tangle of brush, and I doubt you'll be able to tell any difference in the battling qualities of the two fish—for the simple reason that you won't have time to compare them.

17

TERRESTRIALS FOR PANFISH

The use of terrestrials for trout and bass requires a certain finesse—they are intelligent species, not easily fooled by artificials, to which close imitation and proper imitation are essential for success. In addition, although good bass waters are widespread, good trout waters are harder to come by, and in both cases more time is required to achieve action than many beginning flycasters have available.

There is, however, a type of fly casting available to everyone, no matter where they live, frequently within only a few minutes of their homes, that provides both action and exercise in building fly-casting and fish-fighting skills. Although there are many different species of fish involved, the generic term for this sort of fishing is "panfishing," because most of the species only attain a size that fits nicely into a frying pan.

Relatively small size, though, is no reflection on the fighting qualities of these fish, and many of them, given equal weight, will outfight bass or trout. In addition, there is always the chance of a "lunker" panfish going several pounds, and many state records are just waiting to be broken. Because of the tremendous number of smaller panfish, and the voracity they exhibit toward properly presented flies, a panfish that reaches "lunker" proportions is an old and wise fish—and requires every bit as much—if not more—finesse than many trout or bass.

We shall be dividing the group of panfish into four major lots: bluegills; other species of sunfish; crappies; and yellow perch. There are certainly more species of panfish available to the terrestrial fisherman, but these are the most common, and techniques applied to them will often surprise the angler with fish of different species (including small bass) as an added bonus to the day's bag.

The Bluegill

Panfish are not only among the tastiest of all the edible species of fish, they are also extremely prolific breeders. In a relatively small but fertile pond, panfish, especially sunfish and crappies, will reproduce to the point that other fish, such as bass, cannot attain enough food to reach fair proportions; and, in many cases, the panfish themselves will become stunted due to overbreeding for the size of the body of water and the amount of food present. For this reason, the largest panfish are generally caught in "new" lakes and ponds, which have not been in existence long enough for such overbreeding to have accomplished a depletion of the waters; or in rivers and streams, which offer virtually unlimited food supplies and growing room in that the fish can move around more.

Many small farm ponds rapidly achieve the condition of overbreeding and stunted fish, and since these fish compete wiith more "desirable" species such as bass, pond owners are often anxious to have anglers take quite a few panfish out of their waters in order to provide more room for their more desirable species to grow. Rest assured that it is virtually impossible to "fish out" a pond of panfish—if there are enough fish in the pond to be causing a problem, there will be literally thousands of smaller panfish to grow up, fish too small to be tempted by even the most effective lure.

Fisherman's etiquette naturally assumes that you will not keep any fish without the permission of the owner of the pond; but in some cases well-intentioned anglers will return *every* fish caught to the water unharmed. This is a very noble gesture and sound fisheries management in the cases of trout and bass, but actually an unsound practice in the case of panfish, which compete with bass and trout for the food available. If a pond owner asks you to keep the fish, do so: he knows his pond and the steps that are necessary for its management. If you don't eat fish yourself, ask the farmer at the outset if he wants the fish you catch. If he does, clean them for him. This gesture will assure you of an invitation to return. Carry a plastic bag with you for the heads, scales, and entrails, and ask his permission to dispose of the offal in his garbage can—another small gesture, but also one that shows the farmer that you respect his land enough to go to a little extra trouble not to dirty it up.

If he doesn't want the fish, try to keep them alive, either on a stringer or in a bucket replenished with constant changes of fresh water, until you can get them to a river or stream known to harbor that species, where you can release them. Two phrases are important there: *river or stream* and *known to harbor*; never release panfish into any landlocked body of water, since they will only contribute to the overbreeding already going on there; and never release *any* species of fish into a body of water, flowing or still, that does not already contain fish of that species, since the introduction of an alien species can completely upset the ecology of the water.

BLUEGILLS

Bluegills (*Lepomus macrochirus*) are the favorite panfish of young and old alike. They are usually the first fish ever caught by a youngster, but just because they often fall victim to a piece of earthworm on a crude rig tied to a willow branch does not mean that they should be looked upon with disdain by the terrestrial fisherman. The bluegill is primarily a fish of the East, found from the Altantic Coast to the Mississippi and from Minnesota and New England South to Florida and Arkansas. It has been introduced into many waters in the West, especially in California, where it is thriving.

The common size of bluegills ranges between six and eight inches in length, but they are saucer-shaped fish with a very deep girth, and when they feel the hook they fight by turning broadside to the angler, so that he has to fight against the entire side of the fish and the drag it exerts against the water as well as the muscles of the fish in its struggle for freedom.

But, if six to eight inches, and less than a pound in weight, is the rule in bluegill fishing, there are more than enough exceptions to make the pursuit of this small big game worthwhile and exciting. Bluegills

Landflies, woolly worms, and ants are the best medicine for a nice stringer of mixed sunfish.

frequently attain lengths of a foot and even slightly more, and the world-record bluegill, caught from Ketona Lake, Alabama, in April of 1950, was fifteen inches in length with a girth of over eighteen inches, and weighed a whopping four pounds, twelve ounces. That is a bragging size for any fish, including bass and trout. It is record that will be hard to beat, but since it occurred over a quarter century ago, there should be some fish out there that will do it. It is certainly a goal well worth striving for.

Bluegills eat almost any type of insect life that they can get into their mouths—as well as some things that don't quite fit. Mere size of the fly is no guarantee that the fish's size will be proportionate. I have had four-inch bluegills strike a Deer Hair Hopper that I was using for bass, and I have taken ten-inchers on leafhoppers and miniants. Nevertheless, there are certain guidelines to follow for success in taking the larger bluegills.

First, bluegills are primarily a school fish. Occasionally a big bull bluegill will go off on his own, and when he does he usually heads for deep water—sometimes ten to fifteen feet of it. The only chance of taking lone fish such as these on the terrestrials is by using a long leader and one of the wet patterns—either a Woolly Worm or one of the landflies would be best in these situations.

However, the fastest action will come in taking schooling bluegills from the shallows. Bluegills adhere to structure almost as much as do largemouth bass, and this is one of the reasons that you will frequently take bluegills when trying for bass—they prefer the same habitats, eat the same foods, and share many of the same habits.

Bluegills, like most other gregarious fish, school according to size. While there will certainly be some variation within any given school, sizes of individual fish will generally run within an inch or so of each other. Therefore, if you find an area where the bluegills are feeding on the surface, and take three or four that run between four and five inches, you may as well move on: the big ones are somewhere else.

On the other hand, if the first two or three fish are in the seven- to eight-inch category (a good-sized bluegill for any waters), hang on and keep the fly snaking out to them. Three- and four-inch fish are occasionally found in a school of five to six inchers, and the reverse holds true as the fish start reaching valued size—in a school of eight-inchers, there may very well be one or two ten- to eleven-inchers hanging around.

Bluegills are not what one would call shy fish. A boat passing through the middle of a school will spook them, but they will all have returned within five minutes—in many cases, even if the boat remains

Low, weed-choked water is ideal for many species of sunfish, and holes in the vegetation are perfect targets for the flycaster.

171

Open water with structure present is the best place to look for crappies and perch.

smack over their feeding locations! They will also follow a fly much closer to the boat than other species of fish, sometimes taking the lure just as it is lifted from the water. In addition, if they miss the hook the first time, leave the fly in the water. I have had bluegills strike an artificial fly as much as seven times before finally taking the steel.

Flies in sizes 8 to 22 are the most effective for consistent success with bluegills. Larger flies will occasionally take them, but the most action and the greatest chance of actually hooking the fish will be assured by using flies that the fish can easily take into their mouths. Landflies, small hoppers, jassids and floating ants will most consistently take fish, although there is not a single pattern in this book that has not at one time or another accounted for a bluegill.

Bluegills like to school and feed in small coves as well as close to fallen trees and other structure. A small indentation in the shoreline, with tall grasses hanging over the water's edge, and perhaps a grass bed or lily pad bed fringing a space of clear water between the bed and the shore, is ideal. In one such location I once caught over sixty bluegills ranging in size from six to 8½ inches, in the space of three hours. The beauty of it is that this sort of fishing is not uncommon.

OTHER SUNFISH

Although bluegills are the most popular members of the sunfish family (with the exception of bass, which are really sunfish, the true bass being a saltwater species) , there are many other sunfish species that, although not attaining the general size of the bluegill, are nonetheless quite common and real scrappers on the end of the long rod. There is no place in the United States that does not harbor one or more species of sunfish, *all* of which may be readily taken on terrestrials.

Next in size to the bluegill, and second in world-record weight, is the shellcracker or red-eared sunfish, *Lepomis microlophis*. These are bluish-green sunfish, distinguished primarily by the brilliant scarlet edge to the gill cover. The world record for the species weighed four pounds, eight ounces, and was 16¼″ long with a 17¾″ girth. It was caught in Chase City, Virginia, in 1970. The fact is that, although the world record is slightly smaller than that of the bluegill, the shellcracker *averages* slightly larger, and would easily replace the bluegill in the hearts of panfishermen if its range were greater.

Warmouth (*Chaenobryttus coronarius*) and rock bass (*Ambloplites rupestris*) are two similar species often found in the same waters of the East, from Canada to the Gulf of Mexico. Their close similarity is shown in the fact that the common names of goggleeye and redeye are applied to both species. Both grow to slightly less than two pounds, and the chief difference in habitat is that the Warmouth prefers deeper, warmer, muddier water than does the rock bass. Both of these species are more likely to take wet-fly patterns than dries, especially when fished around bridge pilings, boat docks, and rock piles.

The stumpknocker, *Lepomis punctatus*, is a smaller sunfish of Southern waters, ranging from South Carolina through Florida. Locally it is known as the spotted sunfish or Chinquapin sunfish, and is one of the most dully colored of the sunfish family, being olive green in hue augmented by dark bronze speckles. It is found in the same waters as the bluegill and shellcracker, and will often race the larger fish to the fly. In spite of its smaller size, it strikes hard, especially on surface flies, and provides some excitement in that way, although its fight cannot compare to the other fish sharing the water with it.

The long-eared sunfish (*Lepomis megalotis*) is a very common, hard-fighting species, prevalent all over the Eastern seaboard and especially abundant in the states from Maryland through Kentucky. Longears have exceptionally large mouths for sunfish, and are distinguished by the long earflap on the gill covers and the very bright coloration—usually consisting of a combination of bright blue and orange with varying speckles and wavy lines. They feed chiefly upon insects, so are ready marks for the use of terrestrials, and favor large rivers and streams, often fast flowing, over stillwater lakes. Although longears seldom exceed eight inches in length, they are hard fighters—

The White Crappie

as in the case of the smallmouth bass, possibly because of the current common to their preferred habitat, but nevertheless a lot of fun when they start exerting leverage against the end of a fly rod.

Yellowbreast sunfish (*Lepomis auritus*) are most common east of the Alleghenies in the states south of the Mason-Dixon line. They are sometimes mistaken for the longear sunfish, although they do not reach the same size, and are not as hard fighters. They seldom reach a pound in weight, and are found more often in lakes and ponds.

The green sunfish (*Lepomis cyanellus*) is the most common Western sunfish, although it is found all over the United States, especially in the South. It is a pale-colored sunfish, distinguished by the fact that the spot on the gill cover is only on the hard, bony part, and does not extend back to the soft gill cover membrane as is the case in most sunfish. The world record is two pounds, two ounces, with a length of 14¾" and a girth of 14" (one of the few cases in which a record sunfish's girth does *not* exceed its length), and was caught in Stockton Lake, Missouri, in 1971. The green sunfish is a creature of small waters, preferring sluggish creeks and streams, small ponds, ponds, and almost stagnant pools. If one fly in particular is consistently effective, it is the deerfly imitation. Apparently green sunfish are used to feeding upon deerflies as a major part of their diet, for they will hit the imitator almost as soon as it lights upon the water.

The final species of sunfish of importance to the terrestrial fisherman is also the one of widest distribution—the pumpkinseed (*Eupomotis gibbosus*). The color varies quite a bit depending upon the habitat, but it is one of the brightest of all the sunfish, with generally a brilliant orange breast and metallic blue and orange lines and spots, especially on the gill covers. It is a very deep-bodied sunfish, and most often found in schools near the shoreline—it is frequently caught from the same areas harboring bluegills.

The pumpkinseed can provide plenty of action in the form of strikes, and while it is an excellent battler for its size, it is nonetheless one of the smallest of the sunfish species, with a seven-incher being considered large. It does, however, rise to a dry fly readily, and when nothing else can be tempted to strike, the angler out for a little fun can always find it with a school of pumpkinseeds.

As previously stated, sunfish are the terrestrial fisherman's friend. They are so widely distributed that they are available to everyone, and some of the larger species fight harder than some of the more "desirable" fish. They feed primarily on insects, and an angler seeking to perfect his fly-casting skills while actually catching fish will never find a better opportunity than by dropping a fly in a weedy stretch of shoreline, and tying into one of the battling sunnies.

CRAPPIES

Crappies exist in two species, the white crappie (*Pomoxis annularis*) and the black crappie (*Pomoxis nigro-maculatus*). The two species are often confused, and it really doesn't matter which is caught since they are so similar in habits. For the taxonomists in our midst, the white crappie generally has six dorsal spines, and the back has more of a sinuous curve than that of the black crappie. The black crappie in general is darker in color (hence the common name) with more irregular dark brown to black spots. However, although at one time an angler could more or less readily determine the species by the type of water in which it was caught, with black crappies preferring streams and cooler waters, whites preferring sluggish warmwater ponds and bayous, there has been so much stocking and transplanting of both species that habitat is no longer a clue. In addition, the dark, tannin stained waters of many ponds, and the muddy waters of other small lakes, frequently affect the pigment growth in black crappies, so that not even color is any longer an adequate guide to species.

It may seem odd to those anglers familiar with most crappie fishing to find the fish mentioned in a book on tying and fishing the terrestrials, since most crappie fishing is done with either small, lead-headed jigs or with live minnows. However, the fly-fisherman who passes up crappies where they are present because of these general angling methods is missing some of the liveliest action he may ever experience. Crappies —especially white crappies—feed quite frequently on insects, and since

175

they are school fish, when you locate them you are in for constant action until the school moves on.

The trick in fishing the terrestrials for crappies is to be on the water at daybreak and at sunset, and to concentrate your fishing in early spring and late fall. At these times the crappies will feed on the surface; at other times they remain in deep water, feeding more on minnows than insect life.

Any of the landflies, bees, wasps, sowbugs, and other terrestrials are excellent for crappies with the exception of the smallest varieties. Crappies have large but tender mouths (explaining one of their common names, "papermouth") and it is a rare occurrence when they take a fly smaller than a #10. Crappies range in size from smaller than many of the sunfish you will catch to the world-record sizes of five pounds, three ounces for the white crappie (Santee-Cooper Reservoir, South Carolina, in 1957) and five pounds even for the black crappie (Enid Dam, Mississippi, also in 1957). Crappies of two pounds and up are relatively common, although sometimes hard to fool, so be prepared for good fish.

In spring when the crappies are schooling to spawn, work the edges of lily pad beds, and drop your flies right into the branches of fallen trees. Since crappies are among the most prolific of all fish, and will rapidly overstock a body of water if left to their own devices, it doesn't do any harm (and can actually do some real good) to take a few spawning fish. This is also the time of year when the largest crappies will be found since the roe adds to their weight, and if you're looking for a new world-record fish, spring is the time to do it.

Later on in the year, you more or less have to watch the surface of the water for signs of feeding fish, especially early in the morning and near sunset. If you are already prepared with the type of terrestrial that is on the water at the time, this can be some of the liveliest fishing of all. Simply drift along with the feeding school and keep laying the fly where they can see it, and the crappies will do the rest.

YELLOW PERCH

Yellow perch (*Perca flavescens*) are also schooling fish and are found, thanks to stocking programs, all over the nation. Although they do not reach quite the size of crappies, the world record is 4 pounds, 3½ ounces (caught near Bordentown, New Jersey, in May of 1865)—a record that has stood for over 110 years! Nevertheless, perch in the two- to three-pound category are more common than crappie of the same size, and perch do not possess the extremely delicate mouth of the crappie, so they can be fought with greater vigor.

Yellow perch are residents of ponds, lakes, and rivers where the current is mild. Even in slow-moving rivers, they are most likely to be found in deep holes and coves out of the current. Where the water is consistently shallow, yellow perch will take grasshopper and cricket imitations at any time of the day and during any season; where deep water is available to them, the same guidelines should be used for taking them as for taking crappie: that is, early in the morning and late in the evening, with concentrated fishing in the early spring and late fall.

Yellow perch are among the tastiest of all fishes as well as being violent fighters; however, if they are to be kept, the angler is better off scaling the perch immediately and keeping it cool in a creel than attempting to bring it home for later cleaning. Something in the mucus coating of a yellow perch's scales has *got* to be related to epoxy cement! Once dry, they are literally impossible to remove without scalding and skinning.

By all means, take the terrestrials out for panfish. There are probably some panfish not too far from your door at this very moment, ready to give you as much action as you want. Some will help you improve your techniques for other fish; others will just give you a lot of fun and some tasty eating. Rest assured, whatever you want from a fish, somewhere, sometime, there is a member of the panfish clan that can and will provide it for you.

18

TERRESTRIALS
IN BRACKISH WATER

Brackish water is that part of many rivers that flow to saltwater bays or the ocean which contains a mild content of salt. Many of the so-called freshwater fish found in rivers—such as sunfish, bluegills, and bass—are able to adapt their metabolic systems to the increase in salinity of the water, and where there is salt content present as the river approaches true salt water they may still be found. These are areas frequently passed over, especially by bass fishermen. However, because they are a transition area they are frequently extremely fertile waters harboring much food and many fish.

For the fish mentioned above, there is no change in the method of pursuing them with the long rod, since fish do not change their habits sufficiently in brackish water to require a change in attack. Nevertheless, there are several other species of fish—either transitional fish (common in both fresh and salt water) or saltwater fish that move into the brackish waters with great regularity—which may be readily taken on terrestrials, and which are capable of providing an angling experience with the long rod that cannot be equalled by any other fly-fishable freshwater fish with the exception of the salmon—which cannot be regularly taken on terrestrials, and which for most anglers involves the outlay of considerable sums of money. In most states with tidal, brackish waters, not even a license is required (although any nonresident angler should be sure to check local regulations before fishing). In brackish waters the fish can run from a few ounces to several pounds, and many of the fish found in such locales are long, hard runners that will test the mettle of any fly fisherman who has previously been limited to freshwater angling.

The standard tackle mentioned in the section on selecting tackle is sufficient for most brackish-water fishing, although when the striped

A collapsed pier is excellent brackish water "structure" to fish when trying for any of the species of fish mentioned in this chapter.

bass or blues are spawning a rod with a little more backbone may *land* more fish. But, since there are many trout-sized fish available to the brackish-water angler, in such a case the rod should exceed nine feet in length, or the joy of taking the scrappy brackish-water panfish will be annulled. Because of the effects of the salt water and the rough grasses and other underwater structure upon line and leader (not to mention the size of the fish likely to be encountered) an inexpensive level line is called for, as well as level leaders testing six to ten pounds. The casts required are short—seldom over twenty feet, and often much less—and the level lines will perform as well as the tapered lines; and brackish water fish are nowhere near as shy as their freshwater counterparts when it comes to smashing a fly, so that a perfectly turned out leader with a fine tippet is only asking for a lost fly.

In addition to the freshwater fish that are present in brackish water, there are five primary species that will also readily take a terrestrial fly—white perch (also occasionally found landlocked in fresh water), striped bass (which have been successfully introduced to large, freshwater impoundments), bluefish, weakfish, and carp (which are also found throughout fresh water). All of these fish are strong battlers (even the carp, believe it or not), and, if you established freshwater anglers will pardon a personal bit of heresy, will so far outstrip a trout in fighting qualities that it may be hard to return to the six-inch deep

179

White perch frequently reach bragging size in brackish water.

streams you have been used to. Before any trouters write to the publisher to complain—try brackish-water fishing for stripers and blues before you write.

Brackish-water fly-fishing is usually found around salt marshes and shorelines, and is definitely not the place for midges or other small flies. Bear in mind that these fish are used to feeding on minnows and other fish, and although they will take a fly readily, there is no dearth of food for them. Large flies are the answer, starting with #10s for white perch, and #8s to #2s for all the others. Therefore, the landflies, bees and wasps, hoppers, and crickets are the most effective flies for brackish-water use.

In addition to the fish already mentioned, there will be others that take the fly occasionally. I have had up to an hour of action with butterfish, a relative of the pompano, and I have even had hogchokers—a relative of the flounder—take landflies on occasion. If there is anything that can be said in general about brackish-water fishing, it is simply that it is completely unpredictable.

WHITE PERCH

White perch (*Morone americana*) are the brackish-water fly-fisher-

180

man's dream. They are among the most avid feeders in existence, and they breed prolifically. They are found along the Eastern seaboard from Nova Scotia to South Carolina, and are, along with the striped bass or rockfish (a name common to the Chesapeake Bay area), true bass. The world-record white perch weighed four pounds, twelve ounces, had a length of 19½" and a girth of 13", and was caught in Masalonskee Lake, Maine, on June 4, 1949. Larger perch are frequently taken by commercial netters in brackish and salt water, so a new world record is waiting for the fly-fisherman.

Although most white perch in brackish water are caught on live bait, the advantage to the fly-fisherman is that they are voracious feeders, eating anything within their reach including insects. I have personally witnessed a massive flight of locusts (winged grasshoppers) that fell on a small tributary of the Chesapeake Bay that was consumed within twenty minutes by a tremendous school of white perch.

The schooling nature of the fish is of value to the fly-fisherman of the brackish areas, as it is in the case of crappie and yellow perch anglers in fresh water, for, once one white perch is located, a fly-fisherman may consistently catch white perch until the school moves on— which may not be for thirty minutes or more, depending upon the location and the food available. Although white perch will feed rabidly upon grass shrimp, a grasshopper imitation cast over the school will

Eroded marshes are quite often white perch hot spots.

A nice stringer of whites to grace the frying pan.

never pass without a strike, due to the voracious nature of this fish.

As in the case of other schooling fish, however, should the first five or six fish run small—move on. Most fish in a school are of close measurements, although a few that are smaller or larger will append themselves to a school of fairly close size. A ten-inch perch is a very good fish; over a foot in length is excellent. These are excellent fish for eating, especially when fried in butter within a few hours of catching. Since they are prolific breeders, there is no stigma upon the angler who enjoys adding a few fish to the table. In the case of white perch, he could do a lot worse.

STRIPED BASS

The striped bass is one of the hardest fighters available for the brackish-water fisherman. *Morone saxatilis* (sometimes termed *Roccus saxatilis*) is one of the dreams of the fly-fisherman. The world record weighed seventy-two pounds, and measured 54½″ in length with a 31″ girth. Admittedly, such a fish would not readily take a fly of any sort, simply because its need for food is too great, but fish of twenty pounds and above are frequently taken on the fly, especially in the spring when they move into brackish and fresh waters to spawn.

The Chesapeake Bay is one of the supreme locations for taking striped bass on terrestrials. Only the largest varieties of flies, such as the hoppers and crickets, should be used if the angler is concentrating on the striper, since the smaller varieties of terrestrial flies are seldom found where the larger stripers migrate. I personally have caught many striped bass while fishing for white perch with landflies, but most of the fish taken have been in the one- to two-pound category. For fish up to fifteen to twenty pounds, the largest flies are required.

Striped bass are strong fish—stronger than any fish you will find in sweetwater. Any rig designed for stripers should contain at least one hundred yards of backing line, since a striper of over ten pounds will have your entire fly line in the water before you know it. Stripers are *not* selective: a ten-pound leader and one hundred yards of forty-pound test backing are not only acceptable—with the availability of stripers of bragging size, especially on the fly rod—they are a necessity.

BLUEFISH

Bluefish (*Pomotomas saltatrix*) go by many names—Tailor, snapping mackerel, snapper, greenfish, fatback. They are vicious fish (the world record is thirty-one pounds, twelve ounces, caught in Hatteras Inlet, North Carolina, in January of 1972, with a length of forty-seven

Fish in brackish water often run quite large, so some sort of net is a necessity.

A six-pound bluefish that struck a cricket imitation in shallow water.

inches and girth of twenty-three inches) that have been known to attack human swimmers.

It is extremely doubtful, as in the case of striped bass, that a world record will be taken on the fly, since after the blue reaches five pounds in weight it feeds primarily on fish. Nevertheless, the smaller blues, often called snapper blues, provide tremendous sport on the fly rod, and are one of the hardest of all fish to land, due to their sharp teeth, which will cut *any* monofilament line under ten-pound test. A level leader of ten- to fifteen-pound test is required and, although blues very seldom jump, the strong runs and violent battles are an experience that no fly-fisherman will ever forget.

Snapper blues often prowl marshy shorelines in spring and autumn, eating everything in sight. Hoppers, crickets, and cockroaches are the primary flies to use, although landflies and bee and wasp imitations will sometimes account for some violent action. Blues like fast-moving artificials, and in spite of general fishing techniques of the way hoppers and crickets usually behave on the water, retrieve the flies quickly and make a commotion on the surface with them. The violence of both the strike and the fight will more than make up for any untoward feeling you might have regarding the unorthodox method of retrieve.

WEAKFISH

Weakfish (*Cynoscion regalis, Cynoscion nebulosus, Cynoscion arenarius,* and *Cynoscion nothus,* depending upon the species and location) are found on both coasts of the United States, and carry the most common name of sea trout. These fish frequently come into brackish waters, particularly in the spring and autumn, and are voracious feeders at certain times, while almost impossible to tempt at other times. The world record for *Cynoscion regalis* (the common weakfish, and the only record available) is nineteen pounds, eight ounces, with a length of thirty-seven inches and a girth of 25¾″, and was caught in Trinidad waters in 1962.

While weakfish are not the strong runners common to striped bass and bluefish, they average three to seven pounds in weight, and must

A nice three-pound blue taken from a small, brackish cove.

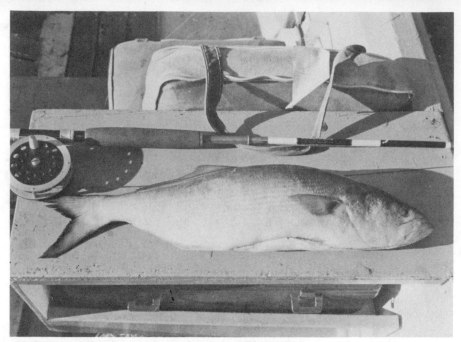

Bluefish and the fly rod are a winning combination for fun and excitement.

In fly-fishing for carp,
twelve-pounders are common.

A twenty-two-pound carp on a four-pound tippet can provide all the
thrills a terrestrial fisherman needs for one day.

Woolly Worms (shown here) and hopper imitations take the biggest
carp, with great regularity.

Two "occasionals" on the terrestrial in brackish water: the butterfish (above) and the hogchoker (a small relative of the flounder, worthless as food but quite a fighter for its size, below).

be played with great care due to the fact that their mouths are exceptionally soft and easily torn by the hook if too much pressure is exerted. Although I personally have caught them on various patterns, the only patterns that they strike with anything approaching regularity are the various grasshoppers—the most effective pattern for all brackish-water fishing.

Although light leaders are not necessary to elicit a strike from weakfish, they may serve a legitimate purpose in keeping the angler from exerting too much pressure, and thus ripping the fly from the extremely delicate mouth of the fish.

CARP

Don't laugh! A carp, once seduced into taking the fly, is one of the hardest-fighting fish available to the fly-fisherman today. *Cyprinus carpio* has reached a world record on hook and line of fifty-five pounds, five ounces, and a carp has been recorded in Europe at a weight of seventy pounds. They fight like a bulldog, and I have had a twenty-five-pound carp on a fly rod for over thirty minutes before I could wear it down enough to flick the fly out of its mouth. Some people like to eat them, although preparation is a bit complicated for the average fisherman. Properly prepared the taste is virtually indistinguishable from salmon.

If there are any carp in your area—and if there aren't you are one of an extreme minority—you owe yourself one of the fly-fishing experiences of a lifetime. Carp are among the largest fish to regularly take terrestrial flies, and I have a friend who, because of tradition, does not wish his name mentioned, who has taken a carp of over forty pounds on the fly rod in a one and one-half-hour battle. Salmon fishermen are rare who can claim such a fight.

Carp will take any of the terrestrials. The best method of taking them is to find a slick of leaves and detritus on the water and to drop the fly into that slick, twitching it periodically. Watch the fly carefully, and when it disappears, twitch the rod just hard enough to set the fly in the carp's soft mouth—and hang on for dear life. I had one carp—and I know it was a carp because I saw it roll—that took thirty-five yards of level line plus one hundred yards of twenty-pound test backing and snapped it at the reel spool as though it had been a two-pound test tippet. Carp fishing with the fly rod is *not* trash fishing—it is one of the most challenging and exacting forms of fly-fishing in regard to technique in existence.

APPENDIX I
COLLECTING
THE TERRESTRIALS

Many terrestrials fishermen will be content to duplicate the patterns given in this book. They are the result of several years of research, and will be effective in almost all of the types of fishing likely to be encountered. However, there are bound to be some of you who truly enjoy the entomological facet of fly tying and fishing, and the close-imitation-school will want to duplicate the precise shades and lengths of the varieties of terrestrials found in their particular areas.

Terrestrials are much easier to study than aquatic insects, and the equipment necessary to this study is simple. A fine-meshed butterfly net will collect any of the insects mentioned in the preceding chapters. Such a net can be constructed at home, or can be purchased already made through several of the companies listed below. The nets are usually so inexpensive that home construction offers no real savings.

In addition to the net, the other essentials are a killing/relaxing bottle, preserving vials or bottles, and a magnifying glass. All of these items, plus instructions on how to use them, may also be ordered from the various companies listed.

The following listings are divided into two parts: sources of supplies for collecting, and various books and manuals that will aid both in collecting the terrestrials, and in identifying what you have collected.

One word of caution: the flytier collects for different reasons than the entomologist, one of the primary reasons being for precise duplication of color. Many of the preservatives offered to collectors alter the color of the dead insect; when ordering, request some sort of preservative that will retain the color of the living insect. Otherwise the time and trouble you spend collecting will not serve a useful duplication purpose.

SOURCES OF MATERIALS

Bio Metal Associates, 316 Washington Street, El Segundo, California 90245

BioQuip East, 115 Rolling Road, Baltimore, Maryland 21228

BioQuip West, Post Office Box 61, Santa Monica, California 90406

General Biological Supply House, 8200 South Hoyne Avenue, Chicago, Illinois 60620

Wards Natural Science Establishment, Post Office Box 1712, Rochester, New York 14603

All of the above companies offer catalogs, and prices are very similar, so in many cases the reader would do just as well to order from the company closest to his own home. However, the catalogs make interesting reading, and some have equipment that cannot be found elsewhere. For the investment of a stamp, they are almost as much fun to look through as the various fly-tying and fishing equipment catalogs listed elsewhere.

ENTOMOLOGY BOOKS

There are many, many books available to the reader dealing with insects, both on the subject of collecting and in general classification and description. Those listed below deal with the terrestrials primarily, although there are a few general books that would be of interest to the collector. Some of the reports on terrestrials listed may be a trifle difficult to locate, but most libraries can obtain them on a loan basis. Other books may be ordered from the various supply houses listed above.

GENERAL INFORMATION AND COLLECTING

Borror, Donald J., and White, Richard E. *A Field Guide to the Insects.* Boston: Houghton Mifflin, 1970.

Lutz, Frank E. *Field Book of Insects.* New York: Putnam, 1935.

Farb, Peter. *The Insects.* New York: Time-Life Books, 1962.

Swain, Ralph B. *The Insect Guide.* New York: Doubleday, 1948.

THE TERRESTRIALS

Alexander, Richard D., and Borror, Donald J. *The Songs of Insects.* Boston: Houghton Mifflin, 1956.

Arnett, Ross H. *The Beetles of the United States.* Ann Arbor: The American Entomological Institute, 1968.

Blatchley, Willis S. *Heteroptera or True Bugs of Eastern North America.* Indianapolis: Nature Publishing Company, 1926.

————. *Orthoptera of Northeastern America.* Indianapolis: Nature Publishing Company, 1920.

Curran, Charles H. *The Families and Genera of North American Diptera.* Woodhaven, New York: Henry Tripp, 1965.

Dillon, Elizabeth S., and Dillon, Lawrence S. *A Manual of Common Beetles of Eastern North America.* Evanston, Illinois: Row, Peterson and Company, 1961.

Ferris, Gordon F. *Atlas of the Scale Insects of North America*. Stanford, California: Stanford University Press, 1937–53.

Stannard, Lewis J., Jr. *The Thrips, or Thysanoptera, of Illinois*. Bull. Ill. Natural History Survey, 29:6 (1968), pp. 215–552.

Stone, Alan. *A Catalogue of the Diptera of America North of Mexico*. Washington, D. C.: United States Department of Agriculture Handbook No. 276, 1965.

APPENDIX II
CATALOGUES FOR THE FLYTIER AND FISHERMAN

The following companies all offer catalogs of fly-tying materials and fly-fishing gear, such as rods, reels, line, clothing, and fly boxes. Some of these catalogs are real "dream books." Often prices are very competitive, so a good selection of catalogs can end up saving the tier as well as the angler quite a bit of money.

Jim Deren
Angler's Roost
141 East 44th Street
New York, New York 10017

Some hard to find materials. You owe yourself a trip to his shop. It is an experience in itself.

Bodmer's Fly Shop
2404 East Boulder Street
Colorado Springs, Colorado 80909

High quality materials, as well as flies and gear. Prices slightly high in comparison to other houses.

Fireside Angler
Box 823
Melville, New York 11746

Good selection, medium prices.

Fly Fisherman's Bookcase
and Tackle Service
3890 Stewart Rd.
Eugene, Oregon 97402

A real wish book. Largest selection of materials, tackle, books available. Superb quality, excellent prices.

Herter's, Incorporated
Route 2
Mitchell, South Dakota 53916

Another dream book. Tremendous selection, good prices. Sometimes out of stock on certain materials.

E. Hille
815 Railway Street
Williamsport, Pennsylvania 17701

Good selection of materials and some other gear. Medium price range, but good quality for the money.

The Orvis Company
Manchester, Vermont 05254

Superb quality, excellent selection. Very high prices. A catalog for the person who wants the best and is prepared to pay for it.

Rangely, Region Sports Shop
Rangely, Maine 04970

Some hard-to-find items. Medium prices.

Reed Tackle
Box 390
Caldwell, New Jersey 07006

Great variety, reasonable prices, good quality.

E. Veniard, Ltd.
138 Northwood Road
Thornton Heath
Surrey, England

Marvelous catalog. Some tools and materials unavailable in the United States. Prices somewhat high by U. S. standards, but quality often worth the difference. Check import restrictions before ordering some materials.

BIBLIOGRAPHY

The following books are divided into two categories: fly tying and fly-fishing. The former will provide information on general tying techniques, the latter on general fishing techniques such as casting and reading water. There are many other excellent books on the market, but those which deal in depth with mayflies and other aquatic insects have been eliminated, since they would not be of any help to the terrestrial fisherman.

FLY TYING INSTRUCTION

Blades, William F. *Fishing Flies and Fly Tying*. Harrisburg: The Stackpole Company, 1962.
> A bit dated in the use of materials, and makes some assumption of previous proficiency. Nevertheless an excellent book by a master flytier.

Flick, Art, et. al. *Master Fly Tying Guide*. New York: Crown Publishers, 1972.
> A compilation of the tying techniques of eight master tiers. Despite the title, one of the best books available for the beginner. Concise instructions and step-by-step photos of *sample* patterns, designed to explain technique.

Jennings, Preston J. *A Book of Trout Flies*. New York: Crown Publishers, 1970.
> One of the classics in the field. An excellent discussion of ants, and chapter on the collecting of insects in general for copying.

Jorgensen, Poul. *Dressing Flies for Fresh and Salt Water*. New York: Freshet Press, 1973.
> Another essential for the beginner as well as the established tier. Clear step-by-step photos and instructions on all types of flies. Some mention of terrestrials.

_____. *Modern Fly Dressings for the Practical Angler*. New York: Winchester Press, 1976.

>The second of Jorgensen's books. New materials and techniques, further mention of terrestrial flies (beetle, ant, Letort Hopper).

Lawrie, W. H. *All Fur Flies and How to Dress Them*. South Brunswick and New York: A. S. Barnes and Co., Inc., 1967.

>Excellent instruction on the use of natural furs as body materials for flies. Techniques can be applied to many terrestrials.

Leiser, Eric. *Fly Tying Materials*. New York: Crown Publishing, 1973.

>The definitive study of fly-tying materials and substitutes. A necessity for any flytier.

Veniard, John and Downs, Donald. *Fly Tying Problems and their Answers*. New York: Crown Publishers, 1970.

>A classic English work on fly tying. Many helpful hints in regard to bodies, deer hair, and winging, several of which may be applied to terrestrials.

FLY FISHING

As in the case of many fly-fishing books (including this one), several of the books listed below also contain a certain amount of fly-tying instruction, usually of a particularized nature to fit in with the tone of the book. These books, however, are valuable primarily for the instruction they provide in learning to cast a fly, the habits and habitats of various fish, and fly selection, except where noted.

Bergman, Ray. *Trout*. New York: Alfred A. Knopf, 1973.

>The basic work on the subject. The paintings of various trout flies are beautiful, but not as effective in determining *actual* fly appearance as are the newer books (listed above) which concentrate on photographic representation.

Brooks, Joe. *The Complete Book of Fly Fishing*. New York: Outdoor Life Books, 1958.

>A good general book on fishing techniques for many species of fish; unlike many similar books, it makes very enjoyable reading thanks to Brooks's many—but short—anecdotes.

Dick, H. Lenox H., *The Art and Science of Fly Fishing*. New York: Winchester Press, 1972.

>An excellent book for basic techniques. The first part, dealing with fundamentals, is the most effective part of the book. Get it from the library.

Heacox, Cecil E. *The Compleat Brown Trout*. New York: Winchester Press, 1974.

>An overpriced book of limited value except to devotees of the brown trout. Mentioned only because it covers the brownie as no book has ever done before, and because of limited appeal is frequently available through book clubs at tremendous savings. The illustrations, by Wayne Trimm, are beautiful.

Koch, Ed. *Fishing the Midge*. New York: Freshet Press, 1972.
> Koch is a superb writer. Tying instructions are also present here, and extremely well done. Ed Koch is the creator of one of the cress bug patterns mentioned in this book, and his instructions on fishing midge patterns are equally effective for ants, psyllids, thrips, and leafhoppers. A book well worth owning.

Livingston, A. D. *Fly Rodding For Bass*. Philadelphia and New York: J. B. Lippincott Company, 1976.
> Livingston has written six books: three on gambling and three on bass fishing, which may give you some idea of his attack on bass. Although Livingston concentrates on the "standard" bass flies— deer hair bugs and poppers—his discussion of techniques and habitat, as well as tackle designed to meet the requirements of bass fishing alone, are well worth the price of admission to a thoroughly entertaining book that contains much of value for the bass fisherman.

Marinaro, Vincent C. *A Modern Dry Fly Code*. New York: Crown Publishers, 1970.
> Marinaro is one of the greatest of fly-fishing's innovators. He was one of the first to realize the importance of the terrestrial in consistent success with the long rod. This small book is not cheap— retail at $10.00—but is worth every cent of the price. His descriptions of patterns could do with a little clarification for the beginning tier, but his description of techniques are clear and invaluable.

Nixon, Tom. *Fly Tying and Fly Fishing for Bass and Panfish, Second Edition, Revised*. South Brunswick and New York: A. S. Barnes and Co., Inc., 1977.
> A very valuable book for the fly-fisherman with no access to trout or brackish water. This book literally covers the rest of the field, insofar as techniques are concerned.

Rice, F. Philip. *America's Favorite Fishing: A Complete Guide to Angling for Panfish*. New York: Harper and Row, 1964.
> A book that lives up to its name. For the angler concentrating on panfish—bluegill, crappie, rock bass, warmouth bass, white bass, yellow bass, yellow perch, white perch, sunfish, and bullheads—it is unsurpassed. Sections on fly-fishing for each species and fly-fishing in general are excellent. Because of its date and supposedly limited appeal, it can often be obtained at a very low price. It is worth whatever price quoted for the angler with limited resources and few fishing holes. The technique chapters which explain fly-fishing techniques for individual species cannot be found in any other book.

Swisher, Doug and Richards, Carl. *Selective Trout*. New York: Crown Publishers, 1971.
> A good book for the trout fisherman. Chapters 1, 2, 3, 11, and 13 are of great value to the terrestrial fisherman. For the devotee of trout, it is a book well worth owning; for the all-around fisherman, get it from the library.

Waterman, Charles F. *Modern Fresh and Saltwater Fly Fishing*. New York: Winchester Press, 1972.

A good all-around book on technique for various species.

Wright, Leonard M., Jr. *Fishing the Dry Fly as a Living Insect*. New York: E. P. Dutton and Co., Inc., 1972.

Although Wright's book concentrates on the caddis fly as the primary pattern, some of the techniques involved in the attempt to make the fly on the water seem alive are extremely valuable to the terrestrial fisherman.

INDEX

NOTE: *Page numbers in bold type refer to illustrations.*